Roots of Division

Uncovering What Lies beneath America's Racial Divide

Curtis Chesney

ROOTED
PRESS

Rooted Press, Greensboro, NC
info@rootedpress.com

Copyright © 2020 by Curtis Chesney
www.curtischesney.com

Cover Design: Tom Temple, tandemcreative.com
Interior Design and Typesetting: Gretchen Logterman
Copy Editing: Christi Helms
Portrait Photography (back cover): Angela Kerr, angelakerr.com

ISBN 978-1-7357704-1-3 (Paperback)
ISBN 978-1-7357704-2-0 (Hardback)
ISBN 978-1-7357704-3-7 (eBook)

FOR PHARAOH CHESNEY,
whose liberty was stolen by my ancestors.

Contents

Waking to Division

I WAS BORN Curtis Warren Chesney in 1980 and raised in Knoxville, Tennessee. Just down the road was a farm where my ancestors once profited from slave labor. A few minutes in the other direction lived descendants of people my ancestors enslaved. Until recently, though, I knew little of slavery in my family tree.

I do recall briefly wondering in adolescence if my family had any connection to slavery. At what age or for what reason, I cannot remember, but I asked my mom. She explained that my great-great-great-grandfather had owned slaves. He had apparently treated his captives well, whatever that meant. After that brief conversation, I buried my curiosities deep enough to forget they existed. They would remain there for a couple decades.

Throughout childhood, I lived on the wealthier side of town, which was almost entirely White. Ninety percent of my entire county's residents identified as White. Only the remaining 10% were racial minorities, and very few of them lived near me. I remember first noticing this separation while playing middle school basketball, observing opposing schools' players and fan sections. Most local schools, like mine, were predominantly White; a couple were predominantly Black. The differences were striking, but I cannot recall paying them much attention. Racially segregated schools were the only ones I had experienced.

While I did have a few minority school friends over the years, there were not many. I suppose I lived in a White bubble, with television sitcoms and movies with happy endings being my primary exposure to life on the outside. *The Cosby Show*, *Fresh Prince of Bel-Air*, and *Coming to America* were among my favorites. Needless to say, they were better for entertainment than they were for portraying the real lives of minorities. The only reality I truly knew was that of White, middle-class suburbia.

My bubble grew when I moved away for college and transitioned into adulthood. I encountered far more of the world in those formative years. My social circles, though, still resembled those from childhood because I gravitated toward people most like me—White, Christian, college educated, and financially secure. That was my comfort zone, and I mostly stayed there through my late twenties.

At the dawn of my thirties, I ventured into less familiar territory. My wife and I moved to Greensboro, North Carolina, the city where she was raised and a launching point for the civil rights sit-in movement. More than a decade later, we still live here today, and we love our city for its tremendous racial diversity. The White and Black populations are similarly sized, making up about 90% of all residents, with most of the remainder being Hispanic or Asian.[1] The full extent of those demographics, however, was not immediately obvious to me. Embarrassingly, several years

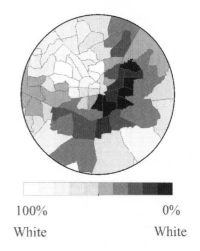

Greensboro, NC

Population by census tract, 2020

100% White   0% White

passed before I recognized less than half of my city is White. You see, like my childhood home, Greensboro is segregated by race, and I was only familiar with life on one side of town. The northwest portion of the city, where we live, is predominantly White with high incomes; the southeast is predominantly Black with low incomes. Over time, I began noticing this racial division in my midst and grew curious about its root causes.

Why is my community still segregated by race? And why do the Whitest neighborhoods tend to also be the wealthiest? Those were simple questions without simple answers.

I found no shortage of differing opinions in news feeds and on social media. Some people said segregation and financial inequality are natural results of free will. To further their argument, they stated individuals can choose where to live, what to learn, and how hard to work. Therefore, if a certain racial group tends to live together, then they must prefer it that way. And if they have less money, then they must be lazy or lack intellect. In short, life outcomes are natural consequences of choices people make, and some racial groups make better choices than others.

Other people insisted something quite different. They said segregation and financial inequality are direct legacies of past injustice. Their basic premise was that White people were favored under the law for many generations, and their descendants still reap the rewards, whereas minorities were oppressed for many generations, and their descendants still suffer.

There were many other viewpoints, too, but the debates seemed to boil down to the same two basic arguments. Racial division in my city was primarily caused by either choices people made or by circumstances into which they were born. Frankly, I did not know which of those explanations to believe. I was more drawn toward the latter, but I had my doubts. *How could consequences of slavery linger so long after the Civil War? Isn't racial discrimination now broadly outlawed? What justifies cries about unequal opportunity today?*

My wife said I was skeptical to a fault. Perhaps that was true, but I knew numbers could be twisted to promote false narratives. As an actuary, a profession focused on rigorous data analytics, I prefer to study facts and develop my own conclusions. But with four young kids and a demanding job, free time for intensive research was limited. I was also nervous to speak up. I generally avoided in-person discussions about race, lest my ignorance or unconscious biases be exposed. Though I genuinely wanted to engage, I was paralyzed by ignorance, busyness, and fear. Hesitant to jump into the fray, I stayed silent on the sidelines.

Remaining there for several years, I observed my multi-racial church fighting an uphill battle for unity, sometimes splintering around racial tensions. There were differences of opinion about worship style, organizational focus, hiring decisions, and whether sermons spoke too much or too little about racial injustice. Conversations about these topics were sometimes derailed by poor phrasing, unmasking racial biases. In such cases, I was bothered both by apparent prejudice and by quick attacks against people with good intentions. Much like the nation, my church seemed to be divided by race. Regrettably, I remained silent. I was disturbed, but not enough to break my paralysis.

Ultimately, I was mobilized by studying the life of Jesus. No historical figure has inspired me toward love and justice more than he. Jesus was a man who defended the weak and went toe-to-toe with the powerful, calling out their greed and hypocrisy. When Jesus encountered hate and injustice, he boldly opposed it. I realized how different we were. In the face of wrongdoing, Jesus was never paralyzed by ignorance, busyness, or fear. If I truly aimed to emulate his ways, I was failing miserably. My inaction belied my faith. That was a hard pill of truth to swallow, but, once I did, my convictions quickly grew, and I leapt off the sidelines and into the game.

In the comfort of a beach chair at an all-inclusive resort, I opened my first book on the topic of race, Dr. Beverly Tatum's *Why Are All the Black Kids Sitting Together in the Cafeteria?* The title drew me in. Feet in the sand, I was enthralled by the end of chapter one, challenged to rethink racism as a system of advantage and disadvantage rather than a collection of individual prejudices. Newly awakened curiosities about social interactions, economic development, hairstyles, and criminal justice compelled me to keep digging.

The more I learned, the more I wanted to learn. I picked up another book, and then another. Some old classics, some recently published. Fictional works. Biographies. Topical studies. Opinion pieces. Podcasts. With little structure, I soaked up information while steering toward minority authors, initially happening upon works by Maya Angelou, Michelle Alexander, Mehrsa Baradaran, Ta-Nehisi Coates, Frederick Douglass, W.E.B. Du Bois, Juan Gonzalez, Malcolm X, and Bryan Stevenson.

I quickly learned our nation is now far more diverse than it has ever been. As of 2019, the Census Bureau estimates 60% of US residents identify as White alone and non-Hispanic. They are the majority. The three largest minority groups are Hispanic (18%), Black (13%), and Asian (6%).[2] *Please graciously allow my liberal use—and sometimes misuse—of racial terms. I am aware they are deeply flawed. If you are bothered or confused by such terms, I can relate. I grappled with the many shortcomings of race and summarized my views in an appendix, called Defining Race, placed at the end of this book. You may benefit from reading the appendix before beginning Chapter 1.*

Though the nation is increasingly diverse, diversity does not equate to unity. The words of these authors forced me to grapple with racial tension outside my comfortable White bubble. Nationwide, average incomes for White and Asian people are more than 60%

higher than average incomes for Black and Hispanic people.[3] There are similarly dramatic differences in measures of wealth, educational attainment, and incarceration rates. And such disparities contribute to sharp racial segregation. Across the nation, money divides, and it divides along racial lines. Work, worship, and leisure are often shaped by informal racial boundaries. Apart from public settings, many people have little exposure to other racial groups. Though we all have unique experiences, segregation is our collective reality.

Our nation, I realized, is more than 150 years beyond the Civil War, more than 50 years past the height of the civil rights movement, yet our wounds have not healed. We are still divided by race. For some of us, the division is tangible, shaping daily life. For others, the division is abstract, difficult to comprehend. People hold differing beliefs about whether racial division results from individual choices or life circumstances, and whether it even merits attention. Simply acknowledging our division, however, does not require us to agree about the root causes. We can start on this common, irrefutable ground: *We are still divided by race.*

With my senses heightened to racial division, daily life began eliciting new emotions. Just after finishing a book about slavery, my stomach turned at the sight of a decorative cotton plant on a dining room table, my mind drifting to the anguish on cotton plantations—battered souls, bloodied fingers, and broken families.

On another day, when a friend carelessly referenced the southeast of our city as the *bad* side of town, it stopped me cold. I had probably heard similar statements a hundred times, but this time I heard it in a different way. I saw the lie for what it was. There is no "good side" or "bad side" of my city. There are wonderful and broken people in every part.

I also realized my wife and I were raising our kids much like I had been raised, with exposure to only one side of town, the wealthier side. One day after church, I took the family on a detour drive through a low-income neighborhood, asking the kids to share their observations. My five-year-old was enlightened by the novelty of a clothesline, and my nine-year-old noticed the many structures needing repair. Around the same time, we began teaching our kids about injustice instead of shielding them from the world's brokenness, and we took baby steps in the fight against racial bias. We added a Black superhero and a baby doll with brown skin to our kids' toy play world. And we sought replacements for illustrated Bibles to correct historical misrepresentations of a fair-skinned, blue-eyed Jesus.

My wife and I made changes in our own lives as well. She started a multi-racial women's group through an organization called Be the Bridge. Meeting biweekly in our home, they shared from the heart, confessed frustrations and shortcomings, and learned from one another, while seeking racial reconciliation. The next year, following her lead, I began a similar men's group. Stretching beyond my comfort zone, I pivoted from avoiding discussions about race to facilitating them.

Three years after opening my first book about race on a sunny beach, I had gained a world of knowledge, but there was still a huge gap in my understanding. It sometimes felt like I had opened a book and only read the first and final chapters, while skipping everything in between. I knew of tragic racial injustice—particularly slavery— that happened long ago. And I had been awakened to today's very real racial division. But I had not deeply studied the many decades in between, so I struggled to grasp why race is still so divisive.

As I wrestled with that confusion, I came to realize the story of race is ongoing and interconnected. The chapter into which I was born makes little sense out of context. Merely learning bits and pieces about history was not enough for me. Until I read all the preceding chapters, preferably in chronological order, I could not understand my place in the story. So I resolved to double down on study time, which would require a major life change. I approached my wife with an unconventional plan: I would request a demotion at work and reduce to part-time hours. Then I would hole up in a library for a couple years until I knew the story of race well enough to tell it to other people. It would hurt my career and our family bank account, but she was immediately supportive, as was my employer.

This book is the record of my study, written as a story about race. It begins where my journey did, with genetics, the shortest chapter covering the longest period, explaining how people separated by oceans came to have distinct appearances. Then it races from the years 1500 to 1850, through European colonization of the Americas and expansion of United States boundaries. From there, each chapter covers a much shorter period, focusing on historical events that explain current racial division. Finally, I relate the findings to my own life, challenging myself with a list of practical steps I can take to promote racial equity.

The most difficult challenge was determining which characters and events to include. If you desire a detailed walk through history, you will be disappointed. I wrote only a cursory review, covering way too many years in way too few pages. To prevent reader overwhelm, each chapter includes only a few historical figures. I also concentrated on the largest four racial and ethnic groups: White, Hispanic, Black, and Asian. Undoubtedly, I focused too much on some people and events and too little on others. And I told the only story I knew, the one limited by my own ignorance and jaded—I am sure—by my unconscious biases. Where my judgment was poor, I request your grace. Hopefully, the taste of history provided here will at least whet readers' appetites for further learning.

Throughout the book, you will find some content, including data charts and deeper dives into select topics, in shaded boxes. This information was critical to my study because I have a skeptic's mind, driven more by facts than feelings. If you are like me, I suggest you review those boxes. Otherwise, feel free to bypass them and focus on the narrative.

Lastly, I want to forewarn you, some incidents in this book are difficult to digest. There were times I wanted to look away and pretend ugliness, including that involving my own ancestors, never happened. But it did, and I committed to writing about it frankly. If we cannot openly discuss the past, I do not see how we can overcome its legacy. This is an uncomfortable, true story, and its key takeaway is rather simple: As a nation, we have traveled far away from slavery, but we are not yet close to a destination of racial equity.

CHAPTER 1

Changing over Time

NEWS OF HIS death spread quickly. Newspapers across the country speculated he had been the oldest man alive, having survived three times the typical lifespan. In the words of a local reporter, he was "one of the most remarkable men on the continent."

His name was Pharaoh Chesney.

And there was more to his legend than just tremendous longevity. Pharaoh had entered the world with distinction; his reported date of birth, July 4, 1776, coincided with the signing of the Declaration of Independence.[1]

Pharaoh's life was a tragic irony. Born enslaved on a day of national liberty, he was forced to labor in a land where freedom was a farce. And my own ancestors were partially to blame for his condition. For twenty-five years, my great-great-great-grandfather held Pharaoh as property. On a hillside farm in East Tennessee, every bead of Pharaoh's sweat fell on my family's land.

Pharaoh's skin was fair, but traces of his African ancestry were still noticeable. So he was called *Colored*, and that was his great offense. Decade after decade, Pharaoh was forced to work without compensation because his shade was just a bit too dark. Under the law of the land, life, liberty, and the pursuit of happiness were privileges reserved for White people. Without legal protections, Pharaoh was told he would die the way he was born—enslaved.

That a man could lose his freedom on account of his skin color made no more sense in Pharaoh's day than it does now. His condition was not grounded in logic. It was mired in the ugly story of race, a story that traces back much further than centuries. It twists and turns through millennia.

Hoping to make sense of Pharaoh's life, and ultimately my own, I embarked on a personal journey through this long story of race. Along the way, I learned a little bit about Pharaoh and a lot about this nation I call home. And every new discovery illuminated my mind until I could finally see clearly. I want to tell you what I learned—about my family, our nation, and the deep roots of today's racial division. We will need to move quickly, though, because there is much ground to cover. The story starts long, long ago.

~

In the beginning, humans came to be. Exactly how that happened is debatable. I have faith in a Creator. Some people believe we were created in a divine instant, others believe there was a big bang of chance followed by a slow creep of evolution, and there are theories in between.

A few basic facts about early humans are relatively clear. Most scientists agree a small group of people once lived in Africa at a time when the rest of the world was unpopulated, and all people alive today descend from those African ancestors. Very slowly, over thousands of generations, these early humans multiplied and gradually spread across the world.

The first big wave out of Africa walked to the Middle East, perhaps around one hundred thousand years ago. Then they spread to lands now known as Asia, Australia, and Europe. Lastly, they reached what we now call the Americas, around twenty thousand years ago, likely walking from Russia to Alaska across land that is now under sea—so the theory goes.

Then something odd happened. Having settled on different continents, the world's population lived as isolated groups for many thousands of years. Like a romantic couple breaking up and going different ways, separated people groups found new interests in new places.

It is said absence makes the heart grow fonder, but not in this case. Instead, absence made the mind grow faint, so to speak. People groups stayed apart long enough to forget one another even existed. Generations upon generations were born, knowing little or nothing of life on other continents.

The longer people groups lived apart, the more their DNA could change in slightly different ways. And the changes were slight, indeed. More than 99.9% of DNA remained identical across all people.[2] But the 0.1% of difference was impactful. For instance, it affected the production of melanin, the pigment that gives color to skin, hair, and eyes. Over time, people closer to the equator came to have darker skin, which naturally protected them from overexposure to sunlight. People farther from the equator came to have lighter skin, allowing their bodies to absorb enough sunlight to produce helpful vitamin D.

That was one of my first light-bulb moments. To be such a simple concept, it had a surprisingly large impact on my thinking about race. I came to appreciate the practical benefits and drawbacks of different physical traits. They were not random or meaningless. They were natural adaptations to different environments. For practical reasons, dark skin would have been undesirable far from the equator, and light skin would have been undesirable close to the equator.

I taught my kids this simple lesson in a recent summer visit to the swimming pool. Per usual, the afternoon started with our family ritual, the kids whining as I cover them head-to-toe with thick sunscreen. A couple of them have my extra-pale skin, which means they quickly sunburn. Through painful trial and error on prior sunny days, the kids had begrudgingly accepted their misfortune, and they usually submitted to the sunscreen ritual without protest. But this afternoon was different. A friend who had accompanied us to the pool was not applying sunscreen, and my kids were jealous. If she did not need sunscreen, neither should they, my kids reasoned. I held back a laugh as I explained, "Kids, I know this seems unfair, but your friend doesn't need sunscreen for a short pool visit. She can play in the sun nearly worry-free because her dark skin gives her natural protection. You, on the other hand, must always remember to use sunscreen. Your skin cannot withstand sunny days without some help."

On a later day, when my kids were not distracted by the pool, I continued their lesson. We talked about how the very notion of race is hard to understand because its meaning changes over time. Today, race has no simple definition. It means different things to different people. And some people are made to feel like racial misfits. For instance, they may not feel White enough to be White or Black enough to be Black. The dividing lines between racial groups are blurry.

But this confusion has not always existed. The basic realities of life were once shockingly different than they are today. Dividing lines between people groups were obvious when those groups lived oceans apart. People across the world barely knew of life on other continents. With few exceptions, they lived on lands their ancestors had occupied for thousands of years.

As the year 1500 approached, life must have seemed stable in most parts of the world. But an era of radical change had already begun. A tremendously long human history of drifting apart was giving way to a rapid coming together. And there was no stopping it. People groups separated by oceans were colliding, with their separate genetic pools mixing into never seen shades of humanity. Before long, people with all types of physical appearances would live side-by-side across the world, especially in the Americas.

CHAPTER 2

Declaring Liberty for Some (1500–1776)

MAJOR WINDS OF change started blowing around the year 1500, and people surely felt the breeze. The new era would usher in conflict and death, as well as human progress and comfort. Happenings on every continent would become intertwined, with some people groups expanding their domain as others lost their freedom. For better and worse, the world would never be the same.

The transformation accelerated on the seas, as improved ships and navigation enabled people to move quickly from continent to continent. Isolated strangers collided together and formed new people groups. It marked the end of a tremendously long era of human separation, and the transition did not come slowly. Winds blew at breakneck speed.

Portuguese ships sailed south in search of Asia. Their ambition was to find an all-sea trade route to replace the arduous journey over land through the Middle East. Traveling around the southern tip of Africa, they eventually succeeded in their quest and realized tremendous benefits. The sea voyage was much more efficient than land travel, and it greatly lowered the cost of trading goods between Europe and Asia, bringing wealth and power to the Portuguese.

But Portugal was not the only nation with ambition. Aiming to compete with Portugal, Spain sent Christopher Columbus west by sea. He, too, sought a trade route to Asia, and his voyage was a true adventure. The crew set sail in 1492, clueless about the length of the journey or the presence of a huge landmass in the ocean between Europe and Asia. That landmass, of course, is what we now call the Americas. The first land Columbus sighted was in The Bahamas, and then he voyaged through the Caribbean Sea.

What he discovered upon his arrival was not the unsettled New World often portrayed or imagined. The Americas, encompassing both North America and South America, was already teeming with life, home to about fifty million people.[1] Columbus referred to them as Indians[2] because he falsely believed he had arrived in the Indies, off the southern tip of Asia. For these people, the arrival of Europeans would soon become a calamity of epic proportions.

News of Columbus's discovery quickly spread across the sea, generating much excitement. Europeans hoped it would bring great riches. Over the next two centuries, they voyaged to the Americas as uninvited immigrants. And they took control. South America was divided primarily between Spain to the west and Portugal to the east, the largest islands in the Caribbean Sea were taken by Spain, and most of North America was split between Great Britain, Spain, and France. It was a total European takeover.

The so-called American Indians were overpowered by advanced European weaponry. Even more deadly were European germs and diseases, such as smallpox, which had not previously existed in the Americas. European newcomers also enslaved some people they found upon their arrival. Due to these many tribulations, in over two centuries, the total American Indian population declined by about 70%.[3]

The suffering soon spread to another continent as well. European empires recognized opportunities for large-scale agricultural production in the Americas, if only they could overcome a major constraint: insufficient supply of human labor. In Africa, they found a sinister solution. European goods were traded for men and women along the western coast of Africa, and those captives were shipped to the Americas to provide forced labor. The slave trade was immense, with complicity spread across many generations and nations. Through the mid-1800s, a mind-boggling twelve million African captives were forced onto ships bound for the Americas.[4] Kept as property, they were primarily forced to work as field hands, producing agricultural output such as sugar, coffee, cotton, and tobacco.

The scale of this tragedy is gut-wrenching—millions of human captives, forcefully removed from their lives on one continent, transported to another on rudimentary ships, and delivered into a lifetime of forced labor. African communities were decimated and devastated, unique cultures and sacred traditions lost. Every captive was stolen for life, without any possibility of return.

They were shipped to the Americas on more than thirty thousand separate voyages, tightly packed in harsh conditions. An estimated nearly two million died at sea. Those who survived were most often delivered into slavery in South America or the Caribbean. Brazil alone was the destination for about five million. Only 3% of the twelve million captives were brought to mainland North America, but that was still a dreadfully large number—approximately four hundred thousand African men and women across three and a half centuries.[5]

From across the Atlantic Ocean, European crowns managed to maintain control of the Americas for many decades. Some regions were even controlled for several centuries. Eventually, however, residents across both North America and South America rebelled and established their own sovereignty. A series of revolutions started with thirteen colonies along the east coast of North America, whose residents had originated from many nations, but mostly from Great Britain. Over more than a century in America, they had assimilated into a new nation, and they wanted to govern themselves. So they jointly conspired to proclaim their rebellion in an official Declaration of Independence. Thomas Jefferson, an influential plantation owner, was enlisted as the author. As it relates to slavery, he was a man of contradiction. He advocated against slavery, while personally enslaving hundreds of people. Likewise, his new nation would profess certain beliefs without putting them into action. Jefferson's founding document asserted all men are equal, with unalienable rights. In what became the most famous paragraph, he proclaimed,

> "We hold these truths to be self-evident, that all men are created equal, that they are endowed by their Creator with certain unalienable Rights, that among these are Life, Liberty and the pursuit of Happiness.— That to secure these rights, Governments are instituted among Men, deriving their just powers from the consent of the governed,—That whenever any Form of Government becomes destructive of these ends, it is the Right of the People to alter or to abolish it, and to institute new Government, laying its foundation on such principles and organizing its powers in such form, as to them shall seem most likely to effect their Safety and Happiness."
>
> *US Declaration of Independence*

Thomas Jefferson

United States liberty was thus declared, but it was not *liberty for all*. At its founding, the United States was only a land of *liberty for some*. In an unmistakable double standard, this nation—my nation—professed, "all men are created equal," while treating some people as inferiors. Colonists asserted their own unalienable rights, and then denied those same rights to people they enslaved.

Deeper Roots
Slavery in the Declaration of Independence

Thomas Jefferson blamed the King for the growth and perpetuation of slavery in the British colonies, as well as the possibility of a slave insurrection. His original draft of the Declaration of Independence included a paragraph about slavery, which did not appear in the final document. In this section, emphasizing select words with all capital letters, Jefferson said of the King,

"He has waged cruel war against human nature itself, violating it's most sacred rights of life and liberty in the persons of a distant people who never offended him, captivating and carrying them into slavery in another hemisphere, or to incur miserable death in their transportation thither. This piratical warfare, the opprobrium of infidel powers, is the warfare of the CHRISTIAN king of Great Britain. Determined to keep open a market where MEN should be bought and sold, he has prostituted his negative for suppressing every legislative attempt to prohibit or to restrain this execrable commerce: and that this assemblage of horrors might want no fact of distinguished die, he is now exciting those very people to rise in arms among us, and to purchase that liberty of which he has deprived them, and murdering the people upon whom he also obtruded them; thus paying off former crimes committed against the liberties of one people, with crimes which he urges them to commit against the lives of another."[6]

US Declaration of Independence, original draft

After studying the founding of the United States, I reflected upon what I had learned. Revisiting history with an open mind, I had developed conflicting feelings about my early European American ancestors. On one hand, I wanted to emulate the courage and innovation that propelled them: Volunteering for dangerous sea voyages in search of new opportunity. Overcoming differences in language and customs to assimilate into a cohesive new people group. Risking death in demanding independence from established European powers. Establishing democratic rule.

On the other hand, I wanted to distance myself from the exploitation and fear that tarnished them: Arriving as unauthorized immigrants with a sense of entitlement. Taking control. Deal making in bad faith with America's original inhabitants. Helping design a massive system of human trafficking for economic gain. Withholding liberty and education from their enslaved captives.

This nation's founders reshaped the world, and I doubt they grasped the long-lasting consequences of their actions. They could not have appreciated how their sacrifices and ingenuity would improve the world into which I was born. I am indebted to them. But I also grieve the long-term consequences of their greed, ignorance, and cruelty. They somehow did not see, or at least did not reject, injustice that is glaring in hindsight.

These realizations caused me to look inward. *What injustices do I overlook today? In the future, when my great grandkids look back on my life, what will they see? Which of my actions will create opportunities or roadblocks for future generations? What government policies that I support will be lamented by my descendants?*

CHAPTER 3

Building a White Nation (1776–1850)

LIBERTY WOULD NOT come peacefully. The United States and Great Britain entered a revolutionary war on American soil, which temporarily stopped trade between the two countries. That included slave trade, which was controlled by Great Britain. As war dragged on, some colonists eagerly awaited the resumption of slave trade, while others hoped slavery would be abolished after the war's conclusion.

The United States did prevail in war, and slavery was included alongside many other contentious topics at a convention to write the US Constitution. Thirteen states, formed from the thirteen colonies, each sent delegates to the convention. The proceedings lasted four months and were preserved in the detailed personal journal of James Madison. Noting division around the topic of slavery, he wrote,

James Madison

"States were divided into different interests not by their difference of size, but by other circumstances; the most material of which resulted partly from climate, but principally from the effects of their having or not having slaves. These two causes concurring in forming the great division of interests in the U. States. It did not lie between the large & small States: It lay between the Northern & Southern."[1]

(future President) James Madison

Division between states, the North versus the South, was an ominous warning of hostilities to come. The greatest support for slavery was in Southern states, which had a warmer climate and an economy more reliant on agriculture. Although most of the total population lived in the North, the vast majority of enslaved people were held captive in the South. Some Southern delegates themselves relied upon slave labor for their economic prosperity. Therefore, opposition to slavery was a threat to their own livelihoods.

The divided delegates succeeded in creating the US Constitution, which settled questions about the future of slavery. There was to be a Congress, made up of a Senate and a House of Representatives, with exclusive rights to enact federal laws. For twenty years, however, there were not to be any federal laws restricting immigration. As part of a broad compromise written into the Constitution, states could admit anyone, including African captives, arriving at their shores. For at least twenty years, until 1808, participation in international slave trade was to be a state right, and many states exercised it. In the last three of those twenty years, nearly seventy thousand new African captives were delivered to the United States, more than double the number shipped to this land in any prior four-year period since the slave trade's beginning.[2]

Then, in 1808, the first year allowed by the Constitution, Congress outlawed participation in *international* slave trade. Shortly thereafter, Congress went a step farther, making such participation punishable by death. But Congress did not agree to a ban on slavery or slave trade *within* the United States. Domestic trade in human captives was to remain a state right.

Slavery was somehow deemed too evil to inflict on newly imported captives, yet too necessary to free existing captives. Though some people recognized the injustice of slavery, Congress did not have the collective resolve to seek true justice.

After international slave trade was outlawed in the United States, the number of enslaved people did not decline. Quite the opposite. Slavery grew because the wombs of enslaved people remained property of their enslavers. By law, children of slaves became slaves themselves, allowing slavery to perpetuate indefinitely. The nearly four hundred thousand captives delivered to mainland North America grew to one million enslaved people in the United States by 1800. And the count of enslaved people would grow by at least 20% per decade for as long as slavery remained legal.

Slavery expanded, though it never had unanimous support, because it always had popular acceptance. Even the nation's most respected leaders were often enslavers. For instance, the first US president, George Washington, enslaved hundreds of people. And he was not an outlier. Of the twelve presidents serving before 1850, ten of them held people as property.[a] Most of them even enslaved people while holding office. Among the innermost circle of leaders, slavery was the status quo.

---

a. All but President John Adams and President John Quincy Adams.

The enslaved population grew at least 20% in every decade.

Enslaved people recorded in decennial US censuses[3]

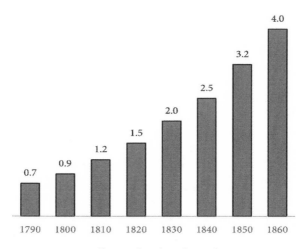

Millions of enslaved people

In addition to allowing slavery, the First Congress made another crucial decision with long-term negative impacts. They legally structured the nation and its citizenship around a concept called *Whiteness*, which generally referred to having 100% ancestral origins in Europe. Socially, some White people split into smaller groups based on the European country from which they had come—English, Dutch, German, and so on. But they were all accepted as White.

The centrality of this concept was captured in national censuses. The first census, taken in 1790, classified all people simply as White or Other, and among people in the Other group, more than nine out of every ten were enslaved.[4] A few decades later, the government changed the Other classification to Colored. Anyone with mixed ancestry, having at least one non-European ancestor, was to be marked as Colored.

This is where I noticed one of many flaws in the logic of race, and, I must say, I found it somewhat humorous. Under the government's definitions, *everybody* should have been called Colored because *nobody* was truly White. That sounds odd, but it is true! Everybody should have been disqualified from being White because everyone has non-European ancestry. As I had already learned, all ancestry eventually traces back to Africa. But that simple truth was not yet known. So, in practice, only if non-European ancestry was recent enough to be obvious did it preclude a person from being White.

The separation of people between White and Colored was illogical, but it was also foundational. Whereas White people could claim the unalienable rights written into the Declaration of Independence, Colored people were denied those same guarantees. For example, the only immigrants who could become citizens were those accepted as White. Other people could still immigrate to the United States, but they were relegated to second-tier status, without the benefits of citizenship.[5]

After founding a White nation, with Colored people enslaved, White leaders embarked on an era of aggressive expansion. Through financial strength, military force, and exploitative deals, the United States overpowered other people groups to increase the nation's territory. There were no set limits to expansion. White leaders dreamed big dreams, bounded only by the ability of other nations to push back. By the early 1850s, the entire present-day continental United States was acquired, and gains for my nation were sometimes losses for others.

One group hurt by US expansion was the American Indians, people whose ancestors lived on American land before Europeans arrived. Sometimes called *Native Americans*, or simply *Natives*, today, many thousands of them were expelled from the Southeast, forced to walk the Trail of Tears to present-day Oklahoma, and then confined to smaller and smaller territory over time. Throughout the 1830s, President Andrew Jackson aggressively pushed for this policy of Indian Removal, contending Natives were an inferior race. In President Jackson's 1833 Annual Message to the nation, he explained,

> "That those tribes cannot exist surrounded by our settlements and in continual contact with our citizens is certain. They have neither the intelligence, the moral habits, nor the desire of improvement which are essential to any favorable change in their condition. Established in the midst of another and a superior race, and without appreciating the causes of their inferiority or seeking to control them, they must necessarily yield to the force of circumstances and ere long disappear."[6]
>
> *President Andrew Jackson*

Andrew Jackson

This was naked belief in White superiority. The president of the United States, a man elected by democratic vote, openly proclaimed American Indian people were inferior. And if they would not yield to superior White people, they needed to *disappear*, according to President Jackson. I interpret this to mean forced removal or extermination. My key takeaway? American Indians were seen as an obstacle to progress, not as a partner in it.

Another nation hurt by US expansion was Mexico, a neighbor to the Southwest. One of the largest and most valuable US land acquisitions came at Mexico's expense.

Just a few decades after the United States declared independence from Great Britain, Mexico had gained its own independence from Spain. At that point in time, the United States and Mexico were similarly sized, and both were young. But the similarities between countries did not extend to demographics. Racial dividing lines were far less strict in Mexico. After arriving in present-day Mexico, Spanish settlers had intermixed with the native people for centuries, and families and cultures intertwined. Mixed ancestry, so to speak, had become commonplace by the early 1800s.

Borders between Mexico and the United States were recognized, but they were not closely watched. People could travel back and forth. Unlike today, the direction of movement was primarily from the United States to Mexico. In large numbers, US citizens traveled west as immigrants to the Mexican state of Tejas, and they gained power. Meanwhile, among Tejanos, there was growing discontent toward the Mexican government. Immigrants from the United States capitalized on that discontent, joining forces with Tejanos and declaring themselves an independent nation in 1836. They named it Texas and drafted a national constitution with laws modeled after the United States; slavery was legalized, and immigrants could only become citizens if they were White.[7]

But the tenure of Texas as a country was brief. After only a decade of sovereignty, Texas was willingly annexed by the United States,

James Polk

further infuriating Mexican leaders. Believing Tejas land still belonged to Mexico, they protested US expansion into *their* territory, and the protests fell on deaf ears. A few months after annexing Texas, US President James Polk declared war on Mexico, with hopes of acquiring even more land.

Abraham Lincoln, a Congressman from Illinois, asserted the war was "unnecessarily and unconstitutionally commenced." Then he criticized President Polk, saying, "I shall be fully convinced, of what I more than suspect already, that he is deeply conscious of being in the wrong—that he feels the blood of this war, like the blood of Abel, is crying to Heaven against him."[8]

Nevertheless, the war happened, and armed forces of the United States were powerful. They invaded deep into Mexico, capturing its capital city and leaving its president with no option but to sign the Treaty of Guadalupe Hidalgo. Mexico surrendered about half of its land to the United States in exchange for a nominal financial payment and, more importantly, an end to the war. In addition to Tejas, the United States acquired Mexican states Alta California and Nuevo Mexico. Territory in those three large Mexican states would later be subdivided across eight smaller US states—Arizona, California, Colorado, Nevada, New Mexico, Texas, Utah, and Wyoming.

When the territory was acquired, it was already home to established communities. Many of them remain vibrant today, still marked by their Spanish names. They include major cities like Los Angeles, San Antonio, San Diego, San Jose, San Francisco, El Paso, Albuquerque, and Tucson, all originally founded as Spanish or Mexican communities.

Reading this history as an adult felt like I was learning it for the first time. To be fair to my childhood teachers, these topics may have been covered in my history classes. If so, I was asleep. I somehow missed how the southwest portion of my country was acquired from Mexico. I was befuddled by my ignorance.

As a visual learner, I wanted to see a full map of the two countries as of 1830, before half of Mexico became property of the United States. Failing to find such a map, I made my own based on information provided by the government of Mexico and the US Census Bureau. You can see my map at the close of this chapter. It is eye-popping. The land acquired, or some might prefer *taken*, from Mexico was vast.

Mexicans, whose homes were on this land, found themselves in an odd situation. Overnight, they became foreigners living in another country. Notably, they did not cross a national border; the border crossed them. With the war drawing to a close, US Congressmen had debated their fate. Would these foreigners be held prisoner, deported, or allowed to remain? And if they were to remain, what would be their legal status? Would they receive the rights reserved for White people or be assigned the inferior position of Colored people? A prominent senator and former vice president made his opinion known. Speaking to President Polk, he appealed,

> "We have conquered many of the neighboring tribes of Indians, but we have never thought of holding them in subjection—never of incorporating them into our Union. They have either been left as an independent people amongst us, or been driven into the forests. I know further, sir, that we have never dreamt of incorporating into our Union any but the Caucasian race—the free white race. To incorporate Mexico, would be the very first instance of the kind of incorporating an Indian race; for more than half of the Mexicans are Indians, and the other is composed chiefly of mixed tribes. I protest against such a union as that! Ours, sir, is the Government of a white race. The greatest misfortunes of Spanish America are to be traced to the fatal error of placing these colored races on an equality with the white race."[9]
>
> *Senator (and former Vice President) John Calhoun*

Much to the senator's chagrin, Mexicans would not be held in subjection, nor would they be driven into the forests. By terms of the war-ending treaty, they were allowed to remain on their land. They were even allowed to become US citizens. As for their assigned race, the government decided to call them White. There was no accurate count of their number because they were not even separately identified in the census. For the next century, they would be simply counted alongside all other White people. They would be outnumbered in a land where English was the dominant language, and they would commonly be treated as unwanted outsiders, but they could stay.

With half of Mexico acquired by 1850, the United States stretched all the way from the Atlantic Ocean to the Pacific Ocean. Yet some leaders were still not satisfied. They believed in a White manifest destiny. As one united nation, they expected to continue expanding both territory and slavery.

The present-day US Southwest was formerly part of Mexico.

National borders as of 1830[10]

CHAPTER 4

Splintering in Two (1850–1860)

RACE WAS NEVER a fixed concept. Lines dividing racial groups were drawn in pencil, and the federal government regularly erased them and drew new ones.

A case in point happened in 1850. Prior to then, any amount of non-European ancestry, no matter how small, made a person Colored. That was the clear line separating White people from all others. But the line grew blurry after Mexicans were deemed White. Including them as citizens despite their mixed ancestry caused confusion. Would people with other types of mixed ancestry also be made White?

The federal government quickly drew new dividing lines to add clarity, and, as was often the case with race, the new guidelines made little sense. Though people of Mexican origin were to be accepted as White *despite* their mixed ancestry, others were still to be rejected *because* of their mixed ancestry.

In the census of 1850, the racial group *Colored* was removed and replaced with two new groups.[1] One was *Black*, used for a person having close to 100% African ancestry. The other was *Mulatto*, encompassing all remaining people with *any* known African ancestry. Black and Mulatto people were counted separately, but they were treated the same by the law. Neither group could become citizens, and neither benefitted from supposedly unalienable rights. Even if a Mulatto person had a White parent, extremely light skin color, and proof of US birth, he or she was still denied all rights reserved for White people.

One such person was Pharaoh, the man my direct ancestors enslaved for twenty-five years. His light skin tone suggested most of his recent ancestry traced to Europe, but some of it also traced to Africa. For many decades, the federal government called Pharaoh *Colored*, and then it switched to calling him *Mulatto*. There was little distinction because, in both cases, the government called him *slave*. From birth, that was the only life he was allowed.

Pharaoh Chesney

Pharaoh's adolescence was spent in servitude to Jonathan Jackson, a wealthy plantation owner on the south side of the Roanoke River in Clarksville, Virginia.[2] There is no record of Pharaoh's father. My best guess is his mother was raped by her enslaver. Tragically, that was a common practice. Without legal protections, there was little enslaved women could do to fight back.

Pharaoh's mother was one of four enslaved mothers on the Jackson plantation, so he had many childhood companions. On playful days, he and his young friends would wade across the Roanoke River in the dark of night. There, they picked watermelons off vines, careful to leave a large stem. With one end of a string tied to two watermelon stems, they would wade back across the river to the Jackson plantation. Clarksville was the home of Pharaoh's youth—the place where he married and raised four children.

Pharaoh's enslaver, Jonathan, had a son who also lived on the plantation. Corbin was his name, and he took a liking to Pharaoh. Gradually, the affection became mutual. Pharaoh regarded Corbin as a "jolly, good-natured fellow," and they spent more and more time together. When Corbin traveled to nearby cities as a tradesman of cattle and sheep, he often brought Pharaoh along to help corral the animals. On paper, Jonathan still owned Pharaoh, but Corbin was allowed to use Pharaoh as his own slave. Corbin's wishes were Pharaoh's commands. In the evenings, Corbin would shelter in a cabin, while Pharaoh slept in their wagon and guarded the livestock from thieves.

One of these trips forever changed Pharaoh's life. Passing through East Tennessee, Corbin fell in love with a beautiful valley near Clinch Mountain and resolved to one day make it his home. When he finally did, around 1830, Pharaoh was forced to move with him. Tragically, Pharaoh's family was left behind. Without any say in the matter, Pharaoh was separated from his beloved wife and children, never to see them again. Many decades later, in his final year of life, Pharaoh would lament about the occasion,

> ". . . the saddest day in all my life came to me when I was told that my beloved wife and children must be taken one way, and that I must go another. A more cruel blow could not have been given to me. I could not have felt worse if I had been told that we were all to be killed. It seemed almost to break my poor wife's heart; and the sad thought has always been with me, whether the poor creature ever lived after our separation. Our four children were grown, and one of them married a man by the name of Jones, who were both sold and taken to Lexington, Kentucky. Of the other three I have never seen nor heard of since we were separated."[3]

> *Pharaoh Chesney*

Living nearby Pharaoh's new home was my great-great-great-grandfather, John Chesney. He managed a large farm property on hilly land. Smoother plains were nearby, but wild vines and thick grasses rendered them less desirable. So John made his living on the hills. He built a mill on the farm and ran a distillery, where he transformed his own agricultural produce into alcoholic drinks.

John was a veteran of the War of 1812. After returning from war, he entered a troubled marriage that endured eighteen years before ending in contentious divorce. His wife's many adulteries, on top of her regular drunkenness, become too much for him to bear. When he petitioned for divorce in 1833, even her own parents and siblings took John's side.[4] Custody of their kids went to John, but his time as a single parent was brief. He quickly remarried and then conceived more children, juggling the challenging daily upkeep of raising a family and maintaining a farm business on hilly land. His business grew, adding an orchard, horses, cattle, sheep, pigs, wheat, and corn to his mill and distillery. Life was full, and he wanted help.

Like many European immigrants to America, John sought slave labor, exchanging his integrity for a fast track to prosperity. How he met Corbin, I do not know, but the two men struck a deal. In 1841, John Chesney paid $421 to Corbin Jackson for lifetime ownership rights to Pharaoh.[5] Pharaoh was sold as an asset away from the Jackson family he had served for decades. The justice system of the day granted John, my ancestor, lifetime rights to the person of Pharaoh—his body, his time, his talents.

From that point forward, Pharaoh's fate was in John's hands. With the stroke of a pen, John could have unshackled Pharaoh's chains. But John's hands, too, were seemingly shackled by the status quo. He was too blind to see the glaring injustice of slavery. Or perhaps he saw it and simply chose his own comforts over fairness.

While enslaving Pharaoh, John prospered. By 1860, he owned nine hundred acres of land, more than any other resident in his county. Pharaoh labored in the fields, growing John's business. And Pharaoh's value was more than just the work of his hands; his ability to reproduce was itself an asset owned by John. Pharaoh remarried and fathered several more children. Like their father, they were all born enslaved with no legal way to gain freedom.

With Pharaoh approaching his twentieth year on the Chesney farm, John stood on solid financial ground. The Chesney family had a comfortable life, one I presume they wanted to preserve.

But there was a growing threat to their livelihood. An anti-slavery movement was rising in northern states, causing angst among slaveowners. Adding to their worries, nearby countries had already outlawed slavery. To the south, slavery had been illegal in Mexico since 1829 and, to the north, it had been banned in present-day Canada since 1834. Yet the United States still considered slavery a state right.

Most northern states prohibited slavery, while all Southern states allowed it. To the west, the huge land acquisition from Mexico had aroused tensions over whether to allow slavery in new territories. Perhaps even more contentious was debate about a new federal law called the Fugitive Slave Act, which required northern residents to return runaway slaves to their owners in the South. Even in states where slavery was illegal, the act made it a federal crime to help runaway slaves.

Understandably, slavery was *the* leading issue in the presidential election of 1860. Candidates debated whether the federal government had authority to determine rights to enslave in western territories, and even in existing states. Some people wanted slavery abolished nationwide, some wanted it extended west, and others held positions in between. Abraham Lincoln, the leading candidate in northern states, held a moderate position. He openly opposed slavery, but also insisted the federal government had no authority to abolish it. Lincoln hoped for an agreeable end to slavery, advocating for state-led emancipation with compensation for slave owners. For people currently enslaved, Lincoln desired freedom, but certainly not equality. He made that crystal clear when he stated,[a]

---

a. During a 1958 debate with Stephen Douglass, while campaigning for an Illinois seat in the US Senate.

"I will say then that I am not, nor ever have been, in favor of bringing about in any way the social and political equality of the white and black races,—that I am not nor ever have been in favor of making voters or jurors of negroes, nor of qualifying them to hold office, nor to intermarry with white people; and I will say in addition to this that there is a physical difference between the white and black races which I believe will forever forbid the two races living together on terms of social and political equality. And inasmuch as they cannot so live, while they do remain together there must be the position of superior and inferior, and I as much as any other man am in favor of having the superior position assigned to the white race. I say upon this occasion I do not perceive that because the white man is to have the superior position the negro should be denied everything. I do not understand that because I do not want a negro woman for a slave I must necessarily want her for a wife. My understanding is that I can just let her alone. I am now in my fiftieth year, and I certainly never have had a black woman for either a slave or a wife. So it seems to me quite possible for us to get along without making either slaves or wives of negroes. I will add to this that I have never seen, to my knowledge, a man, woman or child who was in favor of producing a perfect equality, social and political, between negroes and white men."[6]

Abraham Lincoln

Reading that quotation for the first time left me in a state of bewilderment. Abraham Lincoln, *the* Abraham Lincoln, plainly spoke *against* racial equality and *for* White superiority. I was stupefied. I had been clinging to a sanitized version of the past. In truth, Lincoln *the man* was far messier than Lincoln *the legend*. Compared to prevailing sentiments in his day, Lincoln was "zealous, radical, and determined," but some of his beliefs were repugnant by today's standards. And even during Lincoln's lifetime, abolitionists viewed him as "tardy, cold, dull, and indifferent."[b,7]

Abraham Lincoln

Lincoln won the election of 1860 by sweeping states farthest north and west. His distaste for slavery was so unpopular in the South, however, that he failed to even appear on some state ballots and did not win a single southern state.

Prior to the election, many leaders from the South had threatened to secede from the United States if Lincoln won. They promptly made good on that promise. In the four months between his election and inauguration, seven southern states seceded from the United States of America to form a new country. They named it the *Confederate States of America*, or simply the *Confederacy*. Four additional states soon joined them. The combined eleven seceding states were Alabama, Arkansas, Florida, Georgia, Louisiana, Mississippi, North Carolina, South Carolina, Tennessee, Texas, and Virginia.[c,8] All remaining states, those that did not secede, came to be called the *Union*.[d]

My entire life has been spent in former Confederate states. I was born in South Carolina, raised in Tennessee, and now live in North Carolina. Across my forty years living in the South, I have never personally known anyone who approved of slavery. Those people

---

b. Quotations are from a speech given by Frederick Douglass in 1876.
c. Residents of the Confederacy represented only 29% of the total US population. Seventy percent lived in Northern and Western states electing to remain in the Union, and the remaining 1% lived in vast Western territories, yet to be incorporated as states.
d. Both Kentucky and Missouri were represented by stars on the Confederate flag, but the predominance of their soldiers fought for the Union.

do still exist, but I believe they are few and far between. Today, even in the South, slavery is generally regarded as a travesty. There is far less agreement, however, about the Confederacy. In some circles, the Confederacy directly equates to slavery. In others, slavery and the Confederacy exist as separate notions. I have known people who view Southern culture as an inseparable blend of sweet tea, grits, country music, football, and, yes, the Confederate flag. An affront on any one of those can be regarded as an attack against them all.

Personally, I cannot recall ever owning anything with a Confederate emblem, but I may have. I certainly liked the television show Dukes of Hazard, and Confederate imagery was a centerpiece on that show. Connections between slavery and the confederacy never crossed my mind as I cheered on the show's heroes, Bo and Luke.

In the 1860s, though, slavery and the Confederacy were inseparable. Thirty-nine percent of the Confederate population was enslaved, and the Confederacy had a huge economic advantage due to slavery. Total wealth per free person was nearly twice as high in the Confederacy as it was in the Union, and the gap was growing. In my reading of history, a commitment to protecting this economic advantage was central to the Confederacy's devotion to slavery.

When Confederate states seceded from the United States, they issued official statements explaining their rationale. I read them all, and they forever clarified my view of the Confederacy. Reasons for secession varied from state to state, but the common theme was outrage against federal encroachment upon state rights to enslave. I will give you a small taste.

In December of 1860, South Carolina defended secession by blaming northern states for electing a president "whose opinions and purposes are hostile to slavery."[9] One month later, Mississippi left the Union, stating slavery was "the greatest material interest in the world" and insisting "a blow at slavery is a blow at commerce and civilization."[10] Three days after Mississippi, Georgia issued its own statement, declaring, "The South with great unanimity declared her purpose to resist the principle of prohibition [of slavery] to the last extremity."[11] Four days after Georgia, Texas followed suit. After reminding that the country was built *by* White people, *for* White people, Texas said people of African origin were "rightfully held and regarded as an inferior and dependent race, and in that condition only could their existence in this country be rendered beneficial or tolerable." For added effect, Texas pronounced God's stamp of approval, saying slavery was "the revealed will of the Almighty Creator, as recognized by all Christian nations."[12]

In my reading of the Bible, God is both loving and just. Yet, in God's name, people were stripped of all liberty and made slaves. Day after day, they toiled in harsh conditions without pay. Where was the love and justice in that? How could people's interpretation of the Bible have been so incongruent with my own?

I began grappling with those questions. Frankly, I am still working through them today. Thus far, my biggest takeaway has been that mainstream beliefs are not necessarily virtuous or true. Sometimes they are flat out wrong. I must not be so lazy that I blindly adopt familiar views, nor so cowardly that I avoid pushing against the grain of popular opinion.

After seceding from the Union, all eleven states of the Confederacy approved a constitution protecting slavery *forever*. It declared, "No bill of attainder, ex post facto law, or law denying or impairing the right of property in negro slaves shall be passed." In other words, as long as the Confederacy lived, so should slavery. Its leaders had agreed slavery should not be abolished. Not then. Not ever.[13]

Deeper Roots
Confederate vs. Union Economies[14]

Economies in the Union and the Confederacy were very different. In the Confederacy, the economy revolved around labor-intensive farming. Across those eleven states, 39% percent of all people were enslaved. The Confederacy produced annual agricultural output of $0.6 billion, more than quadruple its annual manufacturing output of $0.1 billion. By contrast, the Union relied more on manufacturing and less on slave labor. Only 2% of its people were enslaved, and its economy tilted toward manufacturing. The Union's annual manufacturing output of $1.7 billion far surpassed its annual agricultural output of $1.0 billion.

Both regions, however, had benefitted greatly from slavery, which subsidized the cost of goods, fueling growth in both agricultural and manufacturing sectors. Commerce related to the cotton crop had especially benefitted. As a share of all US exports, cotton grew from about 15% in 1800 to 60% in 1860. Other countries producing cotton were pushed aside as the United States established global dominance. It reached a point where more than three quarters of the world's cotton was being produced in the United States.[15] And that success helped generate tremendous wealth. From 1850 to 1860, average wealth per free person grew by over 60%, and total national wealth doubled.

But prosperity had not been equally shared between the Confederacy and the Union, and I suspect that was a key source of tension between the two regions. Manufacturing in the Union was less profitable than agriculture in the Confederacy, and the greatest profits went to states most reliant on slave labor. In 1850, average wealth per free person was 64% higher in the Confederacy than it was in the Union. By 1860, that gap had grown to 85%. In other words, on average, free people in Confederacy had become nearly twice as wealthy as free people in Union.

Free Southerners were wealthy and growing wealthier
Average wealth per free person[16]

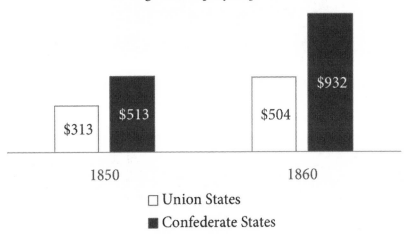

1850   1860

□ Union States
■ Confederate States

...because wealth rose with slave ownership
Average wealth per free person by state, 1860.[17]
Confederate states are black dots. Union states are white dots.
States further to the right enslaved more of their people.

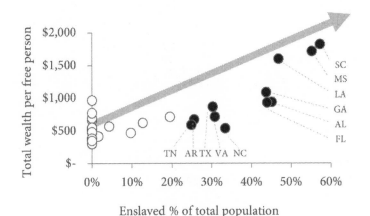

Enslaved % of total population

...and slavery was concentrated in Southern states.

Enslaved % of total population by state, 1860[18]

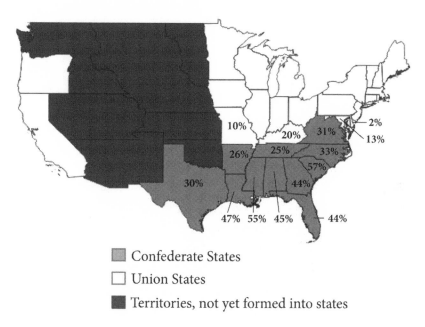

Confederate States
Union States
Territories, not yet formed into states

In states where no value is provided, less than 1% of the population was enslaved.

CHAPTER 5

Beginning Liberty for All
(1860–1870s)

TO PROCLAIM ONE'S independence is an audacious act. And to form a new country by taking land from another is even bolder. That is what the Confederacy intended to do, and they had reason to believe it could be done. After all, they had succeeded in this same endeavor once before. Nearly a century prior, as part of what would become the United States, they had successfully gained independence from Great Britain. That bold gambit had prompted a war, and this new one would do the same.

Just two months after the United States split into two factions, Union and Confederacy, they became bitter enemies. The Confederacy was committed to its independence, and the Union was unwilling to allow a large piece of its territory to slip away without a fight. Through war, the United States began and, through war, it would either split in two or remain as one. Thus began a four-year period now remembered as the Civil War.

Leaders of the two sides framed war differently, casting blame on one another. By the end of the war, Abraham Lincoln, leader of the Union, insisted the conflict had been about slavery and faulted the South for tearing apart the United States. He contended,

> "Both parties deprecated war, but one of them would make war rather than let the nation survive, and the

other would accept war rather than let it perish, and the war came. One-eighth of the whole population were colored slaves, not distributed generally over the Union, but localized in the southern part of it. These slaves constituted a peculiar and powerful interest. All knew that this interest was somehow the cause of the war."[1]

US President Abraham Lincoln

Jefferson Davis, President of the Confederacy, explicitly denied fighting for slavery. Instead, he spoke of a war of independence caused by encroachment upon states' rights, asserting,

"The North was mad and blind; it would not let us govern ourselves; and so the war came, and now it must go on

till the last man of this generation falls in his tracks, and his children seize his musket and fight his battle, unless you acknowledge our right to self-government. We are not fighting for slavery. We are fighting for independence,—and that, or extermination, we will have."[2]

Confederate President

Jefferson Davis

Jefferson Davis

There was no agreement to be found, not even about the reason for fighting. Perspectives diverged, loyalties divided, and guns were drawn, come what may.

In Tennessee, as in many states, communities were bitterly divided even before war began. The question of secession exposed rifts among White voters. Most East Tennessee residents preferred to remain in the Union, but secession supporters elsewhere in the state outnumbered them. By law, the whole state became part of the Confederacy. No law, however, could dictate the allegiance of individuals. After war began, neighbors became enemies, some traveling north to enlist in the Union Army, while others joined the Confederate Army. Childhood friends parted ways only to be reunited on opposite sides of battlefields.

Unsurprisingly, John Chesney's family, my ancestors, took up the Confederate cause. Their livelihood depended on slavery, which was staunchly supported by the Confederate side. Two of John's sons even enlisted in the Confederate Army.

Today, Confederate soldiers have a complicated legacy. Wading through opposing accounts of history, I found disagreement about their primary motivations for fighting. Undoubtedly, they fought for different reasons. But some of what I read seemed romanticized and untrue, or at least incomplete. One such article was written in the 1980s by a distant relative of mine, a fellow descendant of John Chesney. Speaking of John's family, she alleged, "His sons, as many others like them, were fighting for the Southern way of life and against the Northern intruders, not necessarily to keep slavery."[3] Perhaps there was an element of truth in her statement. To me, though, it felt like clinging to comfortable myths in order to avoid uncomfortable truths. In the same article, she also insisted, "Although his sons fought on the side of the Confederates, John had freed his slaves before the war." With a little digging, sadly, I proved this claim to be false. Annual property tax filings show John paid taxes on people he enslaved, including Pharaoh, throughout the Civil War.

Like so many other soldiers' families, John's family quickly learned destruction of war comes in many forms. Both of his sons were forced to return home after contracting typhoid fever, and they brought death with them. Within a year, the sickness killed not only those two sons, but also John's wife.[4]

War raged on, and the mourning at the Chesney home became common nationwide. Death knocked on doors of tens of thousands, and then hundreds of thousands. Mounting losses pressured President Lincoln to find the quickest possible end to hostilities. Any end that retained the South as part of the United States would meet his declared war objective. Lincoln stated, "My paramount object in this struggle is to save the Union and is not either to save or destroy Slavery. If I could save the Union without freeing any slave, I would do it, and if I could save it by freeing all the slaves, I would do it."[5]

Keeping the United States whole, however, was not Lincoln's only ambition. If he could have it his way, the path to winning the war would also lead to the defeat of slavery. As a pragmatist, he also realized the end of slavery would deliver an economic blow to the Confederacy. So he took action—in a way that may or may not have been legal. Over initial objections from some of his closest advisors, Lincoln insisted wartime presidential powers authorized him to literally speak freedom into being. On the first day of 1863, at the war's midpoint, Lincoln gambled his political future on the hope of freedom. By decree, a presidential Emancipation Proclamation, Lincoln declared liberty for all people enslaved in Confederate states.

Predictably, his act was received as an outrageous overreach of power in Confederate states. Even in Union states, his decision was controversial. But emancipation proved valuable to the Union. Approximately two hundred thousand Black[a] soldiers voluntarily enlisted in the Union Army, nearly forty thousand of whom sacrificed their lives for the cause.[6]

Though immediately impactful, Lincoln's proclamation was vulnerable and limited. Courts could overturn emancipation once the war ended because the president lacked authority to overwrite state laws. Only Congress had that power. Furthermore, the proclamation only applied to people enslaved in the Confederacy. In the

---

a. Hereafter, Black includes people identified as Black or Mulatto.

four Union states[b] where slavery was still allowed, Lincoln could not free slaves because wartime presidential powers only allowed him to proclaim emancipation in rebel states. Solidifying and extending emancipation to all states required more than a proclamation; liberty *for all* needed to be written into the US Constitution.

Two years later, in the final months of war, Lincoln pushed for a Thirteenth Constitutional Amendment, explicitly outlawing slavery nationwide. When Congress voted on his proposal, it was a Northern referendum on slavery. There was hardly any Southern voice in Congress because their delegates had left to join the Confederacy. Even so, aggressive political back-channeling was needed to muster up enough votes. Though the North was united in its stand to fight the Confederacy, it was divided over the future of slavery.

This was another lightbulb moment for me. Once again, I realized history is much messier than my childhood textbooks conveyed. Just like I had bought into a sanitized version of Abraham Lincoln, I had misunderstood the North as a place where slavery was almost universally opposed. Even during the Civil War, many people in the North still supported slavery. There were those who owned slaves, of course. Additionally, due to slave labor, people in the North benefited from the reduced cost of goods produced in the South. And there were fears, many fears. Slavery had always existed in the United States, and life after slavery was viewed by some as a scary unknown. Perhaps the economy would suffer, and formerly enslaved people may seek retribution, some people worried. For those reasons and others, many people in the North were not ready to end slavery.

When Congress voted on the Thirteenth Constitutional Amendment, it did pass, but the margin was slim—just two votes. It mattered not. Slavery was to be abolished in all land controlled by the United States. Soon, that would once again include the South.

---

b. Delaware, Kentucky, Maryland, and Missouri.

Just a few months after slavery was abolished, armed conflict came to an end as well. In 1865, Confederate General Robert E. Lee surrendered to Union General Ulysses S. Grant, effectively concluding the Civil War.

The United States became whole once more, but the nation was tattered and torn. Families in every community, North and South, were grieving. Approximately three million soldiers had fought, with more than six hundred thousand dying.[7] And survivors were traumatized, returning home with severe physical and mental wounds. The war also dealt crippling economic blows. Unlike the loss of life, however, the loss of wealth was largely confined to the South. Destruction of farm machinery and livestock was severe in Southern states, where most battles were fought. Economically, war pushed the South back and propelled the North forward. From 1860 to 1870, total wealth in states of the Confederacy was cut in half, while total wealth in remaining Union states nearly doubled. War completely wiped out the previous financial advantage of the South and shifted power to the North. The tables had turned.[8]

With a new balance of power in play, grieving wartime enemies needed to somehow stand together again under an umbrella of democracy. But how? The nation faced an unprecedented challenge with endless unanswered questions. Most difficult would be addressing the status of newly freed people. How would former slaves live alongside their former enslavers? What protections would they require? As free men and women, how would they sustain themselves, starting with the simple necessities of food, shelter, and clothing? Would they be given land? Funding for education? Compensation for years of unpaid labor? Guarantees of legal and civil rights? Opportunities to vote and run for public office? Would people of different races be included as equals in democracy and capitalism?

With so many difficult questions needing answers, national reunification was a daunting feat, requiring a uniquely gifted leader.

President Lincoln was expected to fill that role. War ended as his second term was just beginning, and he was primed for the challenge ahead. Sadly, he was never given the opportunity. Less than a week after General Lee surrendered, a Confederate supporter assassinated Lincoln. Although Lincoln's legacy would be long, his tenure as president lasted only four years.

The divided nation's path to recovery grew even more daunting with Lincoln's passing. In a twist of fate, the mantel of leadership lawfully passed to Vice President Andrew Johnson, who hailed from Tennessee, a defeated Confederate state. As a teammate of Lincoln, Johnson's Southern roots had been regarded as an asset. He was selected to help the nation bridge its great divide. If Abraham Lincoln and Andrew Johnson, as representatives of the North and South, could stand together, then so could the nation. With Lincoln's assassination, however, Johnson's value plummeted. If he was an asset before the assassination, he became a liability afterward, at least from the perspective of most Northerners.

Prior to my recent studies, I only knew a little bit about Andrew Johnson. Growing up in Tennessee, his name was familiar because the Andrew Johnson Highway ran near my childhood home. I knew him to be a former president, and there was some level of pride about him in my state. I also gathered Johnson's legacy was complicated, but I did not know why. Now, having learned more about him, I feel less comfortable driving on the highway named in his honor.

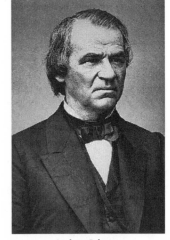

Andrew Johnson

Shortly after being sworn in as president, Johnson set to work resolving the status of former Confederate states. They were trapped in a state of limbo, no longer belonging to the

Confederacy because it had been defeated, and not yet full members of the United States because they had seceded. Somehow, all eleven former Confederate states needed to be readmitted into the Union. Exactly how was uncertain. Unfortunately, the Constitution had not contemplated this situation, so there were no legal guidelines to follow. In the summer of 1865, with Congress away on recess, President Johnson attempted to blaze his own trail. He declared generous terms for readmitting seceded states. They would be required to accept the abolishment of slavery, but they could freely discriminate against former slaves. If states wished to create a racial hierarchy of rights, they would be welcome to do so under Johnson's plan. In fact, Johnson advocated for such a system. As president, he was absolutely clear in his preference for maintaining White control and withholding political power from racial minorities.

Southern states responded favorably to Johnson's offer. They begrudged the forced end of slavery, of course, but they had already accepted that defeat on the battlefield, and the remaining terms of the deal were to their liking. By the end of 1865, every Southern state agreed to Johnson's proposal. Having lost their cause in war, Southern leaders prepared to resume their fight in the halls of Congress. They began selecting new congressional delegates. Among them would be leaders of the former Confederacy, including four former generals and former Confederate Vice President Alexander Stephens. Several years prior, Stephens had explained the Confederacy's core belief in his famous Corner Stone Speech:

> "Its foundations are laid, its corner stone rests, upon the great truth that the negro is not equal to the white man; that slavery subordination to the superior race is his natural and normal condition. This, our new government, is the first, in the history of the world, based upon this great physical, philosophical, and moral truth . . . It is upon this, as I have stated, our social fabric is firmly planted;

and I cannot permit myself to doubt the ultimate success of a full recognition of this principle throughout the civilized and enlightened world."[9]

Confederate Vice President
Alexander Stephens

Alexander Stephens

When Southern delegates traveled to the nation's capital to take their seats in the halls of Congress, they met stiff resistance. Appalled at the idea of so quickly reuniting with former Confederate leaders, Northern members of Congress refused to seat the Southern delegates.

From that point forward, Congress flexed its muscle and wrestled control of the nation away from President Johnson. Over and over, Congress went toe-to-toe with the president and won. By law, there was little the president could do. Congress would pass new legislation with a simple majority vote, President Johnson would veto it, and then Congress would override his veto with a two-thirds majority vote. He was rendered powerless. Despite serving only one term as president, Johnson set a record with fifteen vetoes overridden, a record that still stands today.[10]

Over a decade known as Congressional Reconstruction, Northern members of Congress led efforts to reconstruct the South. To start, they subdivided the eleven former Confederate states into five military districts, each supported by federal troops, an occupying force from the North. The presence of federal troops understandably infuriated Southern White leaders, who had lost their fight for independence from the federal government. Stripped of power, they were demoralized. In each district, military courts were established to protect personal and property rights. And stipulations were placed on repayment of war debts. Debts incurred fighting for the Union could be repaid with federal and state tax revenues. On the other hand, debts incurred fighting for the Confederacy were declared void.

Federal troops also enforced the removal of existing Southern governments and required new state constitutions to be written. Rubbing salt in the wounds, Northern members of Congress could reject the new constitutions they deemed unacceptable. New elections were also to be held, and former Confederate leaders were banned from contention.

Furthermore, Congress acted against former slaveholders. On average, each slaveholder had enslaved eleven people, and an elite class of more than ten thousand enslavers had each held more than fifty slaves.[11] These slaveholders had invested their wealth in human property, and their wealth was lost when slaves were freed. President Lincoln had previously extended an olive branch by proposing emancipation with compensation for slaveholders, but Congress now declared that olive branch to be illegal, prohibiting states from reimbursing former slaveholders. Their wealth had been taken and could not legally be returned.

Congressional Reconstruction also included extension of civil rights and citizenship, guaranteed by the federal government. The landmark passing of the Fourteenth Constitutional Amendment made citizens of all people born in the United States, regardless of race. It also required every state to extend equal protection of the laws to all citizens.

Dramatic change did not stop there. If the Black population were to be truly free, more than just citizenship would be required. They needed voting power. So, brushing the president aside, Northern members of Congress added to the Constitution once more. They passed the final major act of Reconstruction, the Fifteenth Constitutional Amendment, aiming to prohibit racial discrimination at ballot boxes nationwide. And extension of voting rights was not a false promise; it had immediate impact. From the mid-1860s to the mid-1870s, more than one thousand five hundred Black men held public office, mostly at the local level. There were mayors, clerks, ambassadors, deputies, customs officials, superintendents of education, treasurers, and more. There was even a governor. And sixteen Black men were elected to Congress. For the first time ever, Black people were being included in democracy.[12]

Deeper Roots
Frederick Douglass and Voting Rights

The need for voting rights was immensely clear to a man named Frederick Douglass. Born enslaved, Douglass was removed from his family in infancy and tossed between several enslavers over the next twenty years. After multiple failed attempts to escape, resulting in severe physical punishment, he finally succeeded and escaped north. In the lead-up to the Civil War, Douglass rose to prominence as an outspoken abolitionist. His eloquence, combined with tragic personal accounts of slavery, helped fuel the anti-slavery movement. Still bearing the scars of slavery, he knew freedom was not free at all without access to the ballot.

During the Civil War, Douglass established a trusting relationship with President Lincoln, who called him "my friend Douglass" and valued his opinions.[13] No such relationship was ever established with President Johnson. In 1866, Douglass led a delegation of Black leaders to the White House to advocate for Black voting rights. He spoke to the president with conviction, yet strategic restraint, when he appealed,

Frederick Douglass

"In the order of Divine Providence you are placed in a position where you have the power to save or destroy us, to bless or blast us—I mean our whole race. Your noble and humane predecessor [Abraham Lincoln] placed in our hands the sword to assist in saving the nation, and we do hope that you, his able successor, will favorably regard the placing in our hands the ballot with which to save ourselves."[14]

Frederick Douglass

President Johnson understood the context of the appeal. The nation was determining where liberty for all would begin. He believed political inequality should persist and was concerned violence would erupt if racial equality was forced on the White population. Johnson's concern may have been reasonable, but his solution was crude. He proposed retaining racial inequality in each state for as long as their voters preferred it that way. And, of course, all of their voters were White. Johnson responded to Douglass,

"Now, we are talking about where we are going to begin. We have got at the hate that exists between the two races. The query comes up, whether these two races, situated as they were before, without preparation, without time for passion and excitement to be appeased, and without time for the slightest improvement, whether the one should be turned loose upon the other, and be thrown together at the ballot-box with this enmity and hate existing between them. The query comes up right there, whether we don't commence a war of races. I think I understand this thing, and especially is this the case when you force it upon a people without their consent . . . Each community is better prepared to determine the depository of its political power than anybody else...It is a fundamental tenet in my creed that the will of the [White voting] people must be obeyed. Is there anything wrong or unfair in that?"[15]

President Andrew Johnson

Douglass's immediate response was brief and bold. "A great deal that is wrong, Mr. President, with all respect." He soon elaborated in a public letter criticizing the President's logic:

"We reverently ask how can you, in view of your professed desire to promote the welfare of the black man, deprive him of all means of defence, and clothe him whom you regard as his enemy in the panoply of political power? Can it be that you recommend a policy which would arm the strong and cast down the defenceless? Can you, by any possibility of reasoning, regard this as just, fair, or wise?"[16]

Frederick Douglass

Fortunately for the Black population, Congress agreed there was a great deal wrong with President Johnson's plan. So they passed legislation giving voting rights to Black men in the

South. Unsurprisingly, Johnson erupted in protest. And not just in private. He laid his feelings bare in the most public of forums, an Annual Message to the nation, stating,

> "Negro suffrage was established by act of Congress, and the military officers were commanded to superintend the process of clothing the Negro race with the political privileges torn from White men . . . It must be acknowledged that in the progress of nations Negroes have shown less capacity for government than any other race of people. No independent government of any form has ever been successful in their hands. On the contrary, wherever they have been left to their own devices they have shown a constant tendency to relapse into barbarism. In the Southern States, however, Congress has undertaken to confer upon them the privilege of the ballot."[17]
>
> *President Andrew Johnson*

Though the political gains were meaningful, Black representation in Congress never surpassed 2%. The remaining 98% of Congress was still White.[18] Nevertheless, the emergence of a Black political voice generated unabashed White resistance. In the 1868 Presidential election, candidate Horatio Seymour centered his platform on opposition to Congressional Reconstruction. Campaigning under the slogan "This is a White Man's Country; Let White Men Rule," Seymour lost the race but won 47% of votes nationwide.[19]

Many opponents of Black advancement resorted to violence. The Ku Klux Klan and several similar groups were established in direct opposition to Black political power. Their acts of terror succeeded in stopping, and then reversing, Black political momentum.

Early progress toward racial equity was slow and painful, two steps forward and then one step back. The work of reconstructing the South was far from complete by 1876, as the nation prepared for its centennial celebration. A staggering one-fourth of the entire US population convened in Philadelphia to commemorate the historic occasion. In a festive mood, the White population was ready to turn the page to a new era. More than a decade had passed since the Civil War, and they had been years of radical change. Constitutional amendments had abolished slavery, established birthright citizenship, extended civil rights, and prohibited racial discrimination of voting rights. And all former Confederate states had finally been readmitted into the Union. White men in the North were prepared to allow White men in the South to govern the Southern population. There would be no more federal troops in the South, no more acts of Reconstruction.

I paused my studies here to ponder a critical question. After generations of slavery, what would true justice have looked like? Countless enslaved people had died, and nothing could repay their sacrifice. For the four million survivors, though, what could have been granted to ease their path forward? Land? Money? Education? Government representation? Yes—all of that and more. But that's not what happened.

Although there were large gains for the Black population during Reconstruction, there were even larger hopes dashed. Ideas for reparation, whereby formerly enslaved people would be partially compensated, were never considered. Attempts at land redistribution or land subsidies were futile. Major programs of public assistance were contemplated, but scarcely implemented. The White population did not have any appetite for redistributing prosperity. The one large program assisting former slaves, commonly referred to as the *Freedmen's Bureau*, only operated for a few years before its funding was cut.

Newly free people were left to fend for themselves. What was their starting point of freedom? As of 1870, the Black population owned only 0.5% of total national wealth, and the White population owned more than 99%. On average, White people were nearly thirty times wealthier than Black people.[20] The gap in education was also gigantic, for both kids and adults. Only 13% of Black kids were in school, versus 67% of White kids. And only 17% of Black adults were literate, versus 88% of White adults.[21]

That was the beginning state of *liberty for all*. From the bottom of a steep hill, formerly enslaved people would have to climb to insert themselves into democracy and capitalism. America was like a game of Monopoly, in which Black players entered late after White players had already set the rules and circled the board many times. Properties were claimed, wealth was accumulated, and rents were established long before Black players were allowed their first roll of the dice. They faced bitter opposition, and were equipped with little land, wealth, education, or government representation. But they were free.

"Liberty for all" began with nearly all wealth in White hands.

Population and wealth distribution by race, 1870 Census[22]

	Population distribution	Wealth distribution
White	87.1%	99.4%
Black or Mulatto	12.7%	0.5%
Other[c]	0.2%	0.1%

---

c. Represents the only two other categories in the 1870 Census: Chinese and (American) Indian.

CHAPTER 6

Excluding Outsiders (1870–1900)

WITH FREEDOM CAME new opportunities, beginning with the selection of a last name. Some former slaves chose entirely new names to mark their new identities, while others preferred the familiar. Pharaoh fit into the latter camp. Simply dropping the binding possessive from his name, Pharaoh *of* Chesney became Pharaoh Chesney, preserving the link between Pharaoh and his former enslaver.

As two separate Chesney families, they could have developed other bonds. The end of the Civil War was an opportunity to begin writing a new story. John's wealth had been gained through slave labor, and he could share it with Pharaoh's family.

Curious to discover what happened with John's wealth, I dug through family archives and local periodicals. In one article, a fellow descendant of John alleged, "The slaves of John Chesney were treated well and when Pharaoh (or Uncle Ferry as he was called) was freed, he was given land on which he remained until his death . . . A deed giving the land to Ferry has not been found, but it has always been family tradition that he was given the land."[1]

That last line caught my attention. If there was no deed, how did a story like this enter the family record? I had my doubts about its veracity. Serious doubts. Hoping to uncover the truth, whatever that may be, I spent three days in the county records room of an

East Tennessee library. Eyes glazing over, I scoured twenty years of handwritten property transfers on microfilm. By law, all such transfers were recorded. The county ledger is filled with entries of land bought, sold, or donated by John's family, and none of those transfers mention Pharaoh's family. Next, I searched John's detailed estate records. After he died, his personal assets were sold to the highest bidders. One neighbor bought a post hole digger for a quarter. Five chisels and a saw went for eighty cents. Sheep sold for one dollar each, and a large ox for twenty-five dollars. It's all there. Ten meticulous pages record the transfer of animals, equipment, furniture, and books. The greatest prize, his land, was subdivided and sold, with proceeds going to John's wife and children. As for Pharaoh's family, it seems they received nothing. Though they had slaved on that land for two decades, they received no share of its proceeds.[2]

Nevertheless, Pharaoh's family worked their way up. Over their first twenty-five years of freedom, they gradually spent $540 piecing together a ninety-acre farm. This was a sizable sum, but not a fortune. Notably, just a few years earlier, human slaves at auction had regularly sold for twice that amount.[3]

Pharaoh's son Henry established a successful business on their land, growing peaches and watermelons. He even owned horses. Henry's two daughters learned to read and write and became talented bakers, while his three sons joined their father in the fields.

As for Pharaoh, his new life was marked by independence. He lived in a humble, wooden cabin built by his own hands, free hands. Kids came to visit, but Pharaoh lived alone. He could come and go as he pleased, work when he wanted to work, and rest when he wanted to rest. Pharaoh was a *free* man. To support himself, he grew old-fashioned bull-tongue tobacco, selling the lower leaves and keeping the better, top leaves for himself. When customers complained about his practice, he would respond cleverly, "It took me as long to grow the bottom leaves as it did the top." Raising hogs also provided income. He let them roam free around his cabin and on the nearby hilltop, and they would return to the sound of his call. It was said the hogs could hear his booming voice from one ridge to another.[4]

There was time for leisure as well. Walking the land became a daily routine for Pharaoh, carrying his signature cane in one hand and staff in the other. Music was another favorite pastime and one of his many talents. He made his own banjos, and played the fiddle in frolics with local families, both Black and White. Without a doubt, liberty was better than slavery for Pharaoh Chesney.

The same was true, in fact, for most people across the nation. In the first decades following the Civil War, quality of life improved as the US economy soared to new heights. The dawn of this era could be pegged at 1869, with the completion of the transcontinental railroad, thanks to hard labor provided by Chinese immigrants. Though they represented less than 1% of the total US population, they comprised about 90% of the Central Pacific workforce.[5] With their help, travel time from the East Coast to the West Coast was reduced from several months down to just a week, and previously unthinkable load sizes could be carried with relative ease.

The expansion of railroad networks, combined with rapid advancements in farming productivity, virtually eliminated the risk of national famine. Farming produce from fertile Midwest plains could be shipped to people far away. The recipients could even be informed about shipments on newly invented telephones. And if they were fortunate enough, they could make those calls while sitting under newly introduced lightbulbs. Innovations of the era were figuratively, and literally, electrifying.

As overall well-being improved, the gains extended across racial groups. Notably, the Black population achieved tremendous progress in their first generation of freedom. They arguably gained more in thirty years than they had in the three prior centuries combined. Education was a top focus. Black people had been starved of learning and were hungry for opportunity. Childhood school enrollment for all minorities, combining Black people with the much smaller

Chinese and American Indian populations, more than tripled, rising from 13% in 1870 to 44% in 1900. Even adults prioritized education and seized the opportunity for book learning. Literacy among adult minorities increased from 19% in 1870 to 51% by 1900.[6]

Yet they still lagged the White population. Eighty percent of minorities were stuck at the bottom rung of the financial ladder, having no wealth. By comparison, only 40% of White people occupied the same rung. Disparities at the top rung, where people had over three thousand dollars of wealth, were even more stark. That group included 19% of White people and 0% of minorities.

Very few minorities held any wealth.

Distribution of adult men by total wealth reported in the 1870 census.[7]

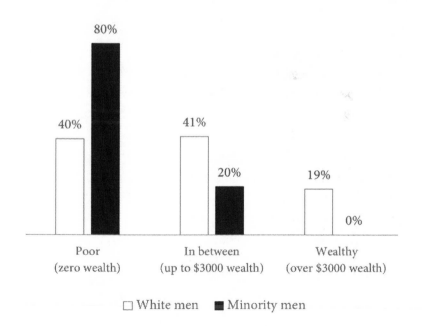

80%

40%   41%

                              20%   19%

                                                    0%

Poor   In between   Wealthy
(zero wealth)   (up to $3000 wealth)   (over $3000 wealth)

☐ White men   ■ Minority men

Deeper Roots
Settlement of the Midwest

Expanding railroad networks created new opportunities in the Midwest, an expansive land area with fertile soil. Settlers migrated to take advantage of generous federal government land grants. The government was aiming to push people west and solidify US control of more territory. Once home to Natives, the original inhabitants of America, land in the Midwest was redistributed to new settlers. It was a massive federal entitlement program. Each settler was entitled to a benefit of up to 160 acres of land, part of a program eventually distributing an astounding 270 million acres.[8] Technically, there were no racial restrictions on the program, but nearly all people receiving land grants were White.

It occurred to me that the land grant program was a huge, missed chance to seek justice for formerly enslaved people. They certainly had the farming experience necessary to capitalize on fertile land in the Midwest, but they lacked an equal opportunity. To have a fair shot, they would have needed clear communication about the program, help with travel costs, seed capital to start their businesses, and assurances they could sell farming produce in a free market, unencumbered by racial prejudice. Without such assistance, this massive government handout was effectively out of their reach.

Deeper Roots
Sharecropping

Farm laborers often worked under sharecropping contracts providing little opportunity for wealth building. Under this system, a farm owner would allow a laborer to use his land in exchange for a portion of the crop produced. Seed and tools could be provided by the farm owner or extended on credit from a local merchant. The farm laborer would work the land and harvest the crop, aiming to produce enough revenue to repay debts and generate a profit. Sharecroppers often faced high interest rates, and sometimes had to work for their former enslavers. In practice, it was extremely difficult to generate a profit.

Farm laborers were further pressured by rising agricultural productivity. From the onset of the Civil War to 1900, the number of man-hours required to produce wheat, corn, and cotton fell significantly.[9] With rising productivity came reduced demand for farm labor. Laborers lost what little leverage they had when negotiating wages or sharecropper contracts, and many were forced to find new occupations.

Lacking education and capital, most minorities were relegated to low-wage, manual labor. And very few found work opportunities outside of the South.

In the North, new labor needs were mostly filled by immigrants arriving in numbers unlike anything the nation had ever seen. Nearly twelve million came by sea from 1870 to 1900, most of them from Europe. As newcomers, they faced difficult challenges, yet they benefited from one major advantage: they were accepted as White.

Too often, White job candidates were favored, pushing minorities to the back of employment lines and lowering their wages.[10]

Meanwhile, in the West, Asian immigrants faced a bitter reception. With the railroad complete, they quickly transitioned from being a necessity to an unwanted presence. California even revised its constitution to prohibit any corporation from employing "directly or indirectly, in any capacity, any Chinese or Mongolian."[11] In the face of such discrimination, Asian immigrants had few protections to fall back on because they were ineligible for citizenship. Their blatant exclusion from society was still governed by federal law, as it had been since the nation's founding.

In 1878, Ah Yup, a man of Chinese ancestry, sought a loophole in the law by testing its definition of White. He argued Chinese immigrants should be allowed to become White citizens. Based on color alone, Ah Yep had a solid case. His skin color was lighter than that of some Mexicans who had already been accepted as White citizens. But the judge failed to see that connection. Without offering any firm definition of Whiteness, the judge said it had a "well settled meaning in common popular speech."[12] Whatever that meaning was, it excluded Ah Yep and all other Asian people.

By extension, the next question became whether Asian people should even be allowed in America. If they could not become citizens, why let them immigrate in the first place? California voters were asked that question in 1879, and they responded in shocking unanimity. More than one hundred and fifty thousand opposed Chinese immigration to less than one thousand favoring it. Hearing their message loud and clear, a senator from California introduced a congressional bill to turn away future Chinese immigrants. As justification, he contended there was an ongoing "Chinese invasion" and insisted the invaders were "unfit, always were and always will be unfit, for American citizenship."[13] The senator's argument ultimately prevailed. In 1882, Congress signed his bill into law. Known as the Chinese Exclusion

Act, it banned all Chinese laborers from entering the country. For the next sixty years, only a small number of Chinese business and government representatives would be admitted.[a]

Deeper Roots
Chinese Exclusion and Senator John F. Miller

White people in California vehemently opposed Chinese immigration and voted in near unanimity for Chinese exclusion. Senator John Miller, from California, explained his opposition:

"If the Chinese are permitted to come and reside in the United States; to become denizens of our cities and the occupants of our lands; if by any action of Congress they are invited to come and form a part of this nation, on what grounds will American citizenship be denied them? If they are free men and are to remain free, and are fit to dwell among our people, will not the sentiment which admits them demand for them all the rights of citizenship? We have a notable example before us. The same reasons which induced the enfranchisement of the negro would be sooner or later urged with the same effect for the enfranchisement of the Chinese."[14]

Senator John F. Miller

Even apart from concerns about citizenship, the senator warned Chinese immigrants would hurt white workers. And he did so while espousing an odd mix of views. He declared Chinese people were a degraded and inferior race, while also asserting they would beat White people in a free market economy.

---

a. The law prohibited Chinese immigrants for a period of ten years. It was solidified by another act in 1888, and later extended even further. Not until World War II, when the United States needed China as an ally, would Chinese exclusion end.

"Temporarily, and under peculiar conditions, cheap labor might be an advantage, but when we consider our condition and are confronted by the fact that the introduction into our country of an alien race of men who perform the cheap labor operates as a displacement of the natives of the soil, man for man, and substitutes a non-assimilative, heterogeneous people utterly unfit for and incapable of free or self-government, the question assumes proportions which are not to be measured by the application of mere economic theories...No matter how low the wages of the white man are fixed, the Chinese underbid him. Competition with such a machine by the free white man is impossible. To compete with the Chinese the white man must become such a man as the Chinaman is. He must work as the Chinaman works, subsist on as cheap food, inure himself to the same disgusting and parsimonious diet . . . If the Chinese could be lifted up to the level of the free American, to the adoption and enjoyment of American civilization, the case would be better; but this cannot be done. Forty centuries of Chinese life has made the Chinaman what he is. An eternity of years cannot make him such a man as the Anglo-Saxon. It is as impossible to bring the Chinaman up to the American standard as it is cruel and wicked to risk, by any experiment, the degradation of the American laborer to the Chinese standard."[15]

Senator John F. Miller

And Asians were not the only people pushed to the outside during this era; all minorities were marginalized. Their very presence in society, let alone their success, was often regarded as a threat, and steps were taken to limit their power. Many people in the dominant White population, viewing racial integration as an encroachment on *their* democracy and *their* capitalism, wrote new rules to racially segregate society.

As a first step, legislators pushed minorities to the outer ring of *democracy*. Voting power was consolidated in the hands of people most like the sitting Congress–White, Christian, male, English-speaking, wealthy, and formally educated. Poll taxes, which are fees charged to vote, were levied to turn away financially poor voters. And literacy tests were introduced to bar less educated voters. Both types of restrictions disproportionally impacted minorities.

On top of voting restrictions, violence was used to suppress minorities. Law enforcement broadly allowed, and sometimes directly helped, factions of the White population to terrorize minorities. The most heinous form of violence was lynching, an act of murder committed by a mob, often by hanging. The 1890s became the peak of lynching activity, surpassing all prior and future decades. An estimated 1,540 people, more than 70% of them Black, were lynched in that decade alone.[16]

Regrettably, the duo of voter restrictions and violence achieved their goals. Black representation in Congress, after peaking at eight members in the mid-1870s, never surpassed three members in the 1880s. Then, in the 1890s, those three seats dwindled to one. All other members of Congress, more than four hundred in total, were White. The political voice of minorities was almost completely silenced.

While being pushed to the outer ring of democracy, minorities were also socially excluded, which effectively pushed them to the outer ring of *capitalism*. Two landmark Supreme Court decisions institutionalized racial segregation. One allowed private citizens to racially discriminate, and the other allowed governments to do the same.

The first came in 1883, when the legality of an act passed during the decade of Congressional Reconstruction was challenged. The act had required,

> "That all persons within the jurisdiction of the United States shall be entitled to the full and equal enjoyment of the accommodations, advantages, facilities, and privileges of inns, public conveyances on land or water, theaters, and other places of public amusement; subject only to the conditions and limitations established by law, and applicable alike to citizens of every race and color, regardless of any previous condition of servitude."[17]
>
> *Civil Rights Act of 1875*

Notably missing from those guarantees were public schools. Included in the original draft, they were removed from the final version as a concession to gain congressional votes. Nevertheless, if enforced, the act would have reshaped society. But it was not enforced. Instead, it was overturned by the Supreme Court. Eight out of the nine justices decided the act was unconstitutional. They explained,

> "It would be running the slavery argument into the ground to make it apply to every act of discrimination which a person may see fit to make as to the guests he will entertain, or as to the people he will take into his coach or cab or car, or admit to his concert or theatre, or deal with in other matters of intercourse or business."[18]
>
> *Supreme Court majority opinion, 1883*

With this ruling, the courts permitted businesses to racially discriminate as they pleased. The White majority could legally structure the economy around itself, making minorities outsiders. Based on race alone, employees could be fired. Business owners could be denied supplies or starved of consumers. Banks could choose who to serve and who to reject. Restaurants and entertainment venues could create separate seating sections. In short, by the law of the land, minorities were socially excluded and economically disadvantaged.

The 1883 ruling, however, only allowed private actors to discriminate. Whether governments could do the same was unclear. State legislators tested their rights to discriminate by passing new laws forcing segregation on their citizens. Notably, Louisiana enacted a law requiring railway companies to "provide equal, but separate, accommodations for the white and colored races." Even if railway companies preferred integrated seating, they were legally forced to segregate all passengers.[19]

Opponents of the Louisiana law orchestrated a test case challenging the law's constitutionality. A man named Homer Plessy agreed to intentionally break the law and have a lawsuit brought on his behalf. Plessy was a compelling case because he was legally Black yet had light skin color, allowing him to sometimes pass as White. Only one of his eight great-grandparents was Black, the other seven being White. The event had to be carefully planned to ensure the light-skinned Plessy was even noticed, and the plan worked. After taking a seat in the Whites-only section, Plessy was instructed to move, he refused, and was arrested. As intended, the ensuing legal case made its way to the Supreme Court.

The final ruling, however, was not as hoped. In a seven-to-one decision, the all-White panel of justices ruled against Plessy and upheld government-mandated segregation. Defending the law, the majority opinion said,

> "We think the enforced separation of the races, as applied to the internal commerce of the State, neither abridges the privileges or immunities of the colored man, deprives him of his property without due process of law, nor denies

him the equal protection of the laws within the meaning of the Fourteenth Amendment . . . We consider the underlying fallacy of the plaintiff's argument to consist in the assumption that the enforced separation of the two races stamps the colored race with a badge of inferiority. If this be so, it is not by reason of anything found in the act, but solely because the colored race chooses to put that construction upon it."[20]

Supreme Court majority opinion, 1896

The lone dissenting Supreme Court justice was frank in opposition. He appealed,

"If a white man and a black man choose to occupy the same public conveyance on a public highway, it is their right to do so, and no government, proceeding alone on grounds of race, can prevent it without infringing the personal liberty of each . . . What can more certainly arouse race hate, what more certainly create and perpetuate a feeling of distrust between these races, than state enactments which, in fact, proceed on the ground that colored citizens are so inferior and degraded that they cannot be allowed to sit in public coaches occupied by white citizens. That, as all will admit, is the real meaning of such legislation as was enacted in Louisiana."[21]

John Marshall Harlan
Supreme Court dissenting opinion, 1896

Among minorities, responses to such egregious injustices were as varied as people are unique. Some risked their lives demanding immediate equality and opposing voter restrictions, lynching, and forced segregation. Others accepted their place outside the inner circle as an uncontrollable reality and chose to focus on matters they deemed controllable. The most prominent Black leader of the era, Booker T. Washington, fit into the latter camp.

Like Pharaoh Chesney, Frederick Douglass, and so many others, Washington was born enslaved to a Black mother and an absent White father. He faced more than his fair share of adversity, but if he harbored any resentment, it rarely showed. In a characteristic statement, he once declared, "Success is to be measured not so much by the position that one has reached in life as by the obstacles which he has overcome while trying to succeed."[22]

Booker T. Washington

A tireless worker and champion of the dignity of labor, Washington devoted his life to the betterment of the Black population. He hoped for equal voting rights and an end to racial discrimination, but those aims were not the center of his work. Rather, he focused on improving the contributions Black people provided to their local communities, believing the eventual result would be racial equity. With unwavering optimism, he noted,

> "Despite superficial and temporary signs which might lead one to entertain a contrary opinion, there was never a time when I felt more hopeful for the race than I do at the present. The great human law that in the end recognizes and rewards merit is everlasting and universal. The outside world does not know, neither can it appreciate, the struggle that is constantly going on in the hearts of both the Southern white people and their former slaves to free themselves from racial prejudice."[23]
>
> *Booker T. Washington*

At the helm of a leading Black educational institution, Tuskegee Institute, Washington rose to national prominence. Put him on a stage, and he could draw a crowd of any race. Near the close of the 1800s, Washington delivered his most famous speech, now referred to as the *Atlanta Compromise*, which influenced national policies and sparked controversy for decades. Speaking to a White audience in Atlanta, Georgia, he conceded social segregation, while also appealing for educational support,

> "As we have proved our loyalty to you in the past, in nursing your children, watching by the sick-bed of your mothers and fathers, and often following them with tear-dimmed eyes to their graves, so in the future, in our humble way, we shall stand by you with a devotion that no foreigner can approach, ready to lay down our lives, if need be, in defence of yours, interlacing our industrial, commercial, civil, and religious life with yours in a way that shall make the interests of both races one. *In all things that are purely social we can be as separate as the fingers*, yet one as the hand in all things essential to mutual progress. There is no defence or security for any of us except in the highest intelligence and development of all. If anywhere there are efforts tending to curtail the fullest growth of the Negro, let these efforts be turned into stimulating, encouraging, and making him the most useful and intelligent citizen. Effort or means so invested will pay a thousand percent interest."[24]
>
> *Booker T. Washington*

Though Washington's speech covered many topics, one line reverberated the loudest: "In all things that are purely social, we can be as separate as the fingers." To his White listeners, this was heard as a giant concession and the last of an important trio to fall into place. With the century about to turn, racial segregation was supported by White leaders, legally approved by the Supreme Court, and now publicly conceded by the foremost Black leader. The terms of racial separation had effectively been set. Minorities could educate themselves and retain their freedom from slavery, but forced segregation and discrimination would be allowed, and minorities would be expected to respect White social customs. If those customs kept minorities as outsiders, then outsiders they would be.

CHAPTER 7

Entrenching Bias (1900–1930)

MY PERSPECTIVE ON time changes as I age. As a child, a month felt like an eternity to wait for an exciting event. By the time I reached high school, months passed quickly, but semesters still seemed long. I approached every year of adolescence as an entirely different era of life. Now, at the halfway mark of life expectancy, I have a new frame of reference. Time seems to pass more quickly, and life phases are separated by decades rather than years.

Researching for this book similarly changed the way I think about our nation's history. I realized the duration of our nation is just a blink of an eye relative to the length of human history. A century is so brief, I can nearly reach back and touch the early 1900s. My grandparents were born in that era. The house I recently owned was built in that era. And, incredibly, Pharaoh was still alive in that era. As the century turned, Pharaoh was reportedly over 120 years old. Without birth records, this incredible claim is questionable, but the more important point is indisputable: he lived a full lifetime as a slave, followed by another full lifetime as a free man.

Pharaoh and his nation, having spent their entire lives together, had walked the same troubled path from slavery toward equity. They covered some ground, but their journey was far from complete. Natives and Mexicans had been cast aside as the United States expanded west and south. On a foundation of slavery, fortunes had been earned, freedoms lost, and families splintered. And liberty was finally extended to all through a bloody Civil War. Yet prosperity gained through slavery was not shared with newly freed men and women. And people not accepted as White were made outsiders on account of their race.

As possibly the only person who had experienced this entire history of the nation, Pharaoh became a local legend. In 1902, he agreed to meet with a professor from the University of Tennessee and reminisce about his long life. Their discussion bounced between many topics. Pharaoh talked wistfully about his childhood in Virginia, grieved the loss of his family when he was taken to Tennessee, bantered about historic weather events, and recalled several encounters with Natives, or "savages," as he knew them.

As he sat with the professor, Pharaoh must have known death was near, and it did not bother him. In a vulnerable moment, he confided,

> "I feel that I have now nothing to live for, and am simply waiting for my Master's call; and when that summons shall come, that same sustaining faith whispers to me, that perchance some of those loved ones have already gone on before me, and may be the first to greet me over there. That ever-abiding faith in my Creator's power and wisdom also assures me that though my bones are not buried at my old Virginia home—as my most cherished wish has been—that when the great roll-call of heaven is made, that here in Sunny Tennessee, my grave will be found by Him, and I shall awake and come forth and enter upon that new life, which shall know neither decay nor death, and where severed ties and dismembered families will enter upon a perpetual union, 'Where the wicked cease from troubling and the weary be at rest.'"[1]
>
> *Pharaoh Chesney*

Within a few months of speaking these words, Pharaoh died alone in his humble Tennessee cabin. Days passed before his lifeless body was even discovered. Though eating "poisoned greens" was the reported cause of death, I suspect his body simply had nothing left to give. His days were done.

In Pharaoh's absence, the nation's long journey from slavery toward equity would continue, and the distance left to travel was great. The pace of progress was slow, and there were no signs of a quickening.

Just one year before Pharaoh's death, Booker T. Washington had learned the consequences of moving too fast toward equity. White leaders valued Washington as a political ally, but their embrace had strict limits; Washington was expected to maintain separation between races. When he crossed an uncrossable line, in the nation's highest house, with its highest leader, there was a fierce White backlash.

The event was triggered when President Theodore (Teddy) Roosevelt, seemingly with little forethought, invited Washington to dine at the White House. Other Black US leaders had visited the nation's most esteemed home, but none had ever been welcomed for dinner. Washington accepted the invitation and dined with the president's family.

Theodore Roosevelt

A prominent Black man sharing a meal with the nation's leading family gave the appearance of radical progress toward racial equality—too much, in the minds of many. Instead of inspiring progress, the dinner sparked outrage. In popular press coverage, the fury was not unanimous, but it was widespread and vicious, particularly in the South.

Roosevelt was sharply criticized. A Tennessee newspaper called the dinner "the most damnable outrage which has ever been perpetrated by any citizen of the United States."[2] A Louisiana newspaper declared, "The Negro is not the social equal of the white man. Social equality between the white race and the black race has never existed and never will exist. It is the decision of the ages; and Mr. Roosevelt might as well attempt to rub the stars out of the firmament as to try to erase that conviction from the heart and brain of the American people."[3]

Many other attacks referred to Washington as a "nigger," a hateful term asserting inferiority of people with African ancestry. A Senator from South Carolina[a] proclaimed, "The action of President Roosevelt in entertaining that nigger will necessitate our killing a thousand niggers in the South before they will learn their place again."[4] The soon-to-be Governor of Mississippi[b] said the White House was "so saturated with the odor of nigger that the rats have taken refuge in the stable," and he promised, "Mississippi is not going to let niggers hold office."[5] A Missouri newspaper even published a poem entitled "Niggers in the White House." Its closing stanzas stoked fears that racially integrated social events would lead to racially integrated marriages:

> There is trouble in the White House, more than you can tell.
> Yelling like wild men, niggers raising hell.
> I see a way to settle it, just as clear as water –
> let Mr. Booker Washington marry Teddy's daughter.
> Or if this does not overflow Teddy's cup of joy,
> then let Miss Dinah Washington marry Teddy's boy.
> But everything is settled: Roosevelt is dead.
> Niggers in the White House cut off Teddy's head.
>   *Poem "Niggers in the White House"*[6]

a. Senator Benjamin Tillman
b. Governor James Vardaman

Both President Roosevelt and Booker T. Washington were accused of committing social treason. President Roosevelt defended the dinner, asserting he would not let public outcry prevent any such future invitations. Yet, in his remaining seven years in office, he never again invited a Black dinner guest to the White House.

As for Washington, he tried to stay clear of the debate. When he did address the matter, he walked a fine line, defending the dinner without backtracking on his prior concessions. Because the dinner had occurred in a Northern city, he argued, Southern customs had not been disrespected. Further, he advocated respect for social customs rooted in racial prejudice, arguing that "it does not pay to disturb" such practices. He also committed to avoiding any actions that would "provoke bitterness between the races or misunderstanding between the North and the South."[7]

Washington's posture may have served a strategic purpose, but it drew the ire of a rising tide of Black leaders who preferred a less conciliatory approach. In the first decade of the 1900s, one especially articulate and candid leader rose to prominence with an anti-Washington message. That leader was William Edward Burghardt Du Bois, more commonly called W.E.B. Du Bois.

Born just a few years after the Civil War, Du Bois was part of a new generation who had never known slavery, but also had never experienced equality. Forty years had passed since the Emancipation Proclamation, and he was exasperated by the continued second tier status of the Black population.

Du Bois called for open-minded criticism of wrongdoing, regardless of who committed it, and he practiced what he preached. Speaking about

W. E. B. Du Bois

the decade following emancipation, Du Bois said there were two great obstacles, the tyrant and the idler, or the "slaveholder who was determined to perpetuate slavery under another name" and "the freedman who regarded freedom as perpetual rest."[8]

Some of his sharpest criticisms were levied against Booker T. Washington, whose philosophies he regarded as seeds that would inevitably produce "a harvest of disaster to our children, black and white."[9] In regard to Washington's temporary concession of voting rights, or suffrage, Du Bois declared, "He is striving nobly to make Negro artisans business men and property-owners; but it is utterly impossible, under modern competitive methods, for workingmen and property-owners to defend their rights and exist without the right of suffrage."[10] When Du Bois published those words in 1903, his concerns were justified. The count of Black members of Congress had just decreased from one to zero. All 447 sitting members of Congress were White men, meaning no minorities could vote on federal legislation. Not even one.

Among Du Bois's concerns, segregation was perhaps the greatest. After the 1890s Supreme Court decision against Homer Plessy, state legislatures had continued oppressing minorities, and racial bias was entrenching. The early 1900s is generally regarded as the peak of Jim Crow laws, a varied collection of state and local laws mandating racial segregation. Believing those laws had grave consequences, Du Bois warned,

> "There is almost no community of intellectual life or point of transference where the thoughts and feelings of one race can come into direct contact and sympathy with the thoughts and feelings of the other . . . They go to separate churches, they live in separate sections, they are strictly separated in all public gatherings, they travel separately, and they are beginning to read different papers and books. To most libraries, lectures, concerts,

and museums, Negroes are either not admitted at all, or on terms peculiarly galling to the pride of the very classes who might otherwise be attracted . . . it is usually true the very representatives of the two races, who for mutual benefit and the welfare of the land ought to be in complete understanding and sympathy, are so far strangers that one side thinks all whites are narrow and prejudiced, and the other thinks educated Negroes dangerous and insolent."[11]

W.E.B Du Bois

Troubled by the trajectory of the nation and frustrated by Booker T. Washington's reluctance to publicly oppose segregation, Du Bois published an essay arguing against many of Washington's ideas. Closing with an impassioned plea for Black men to accept nothing less than equality as set forth by the Declaration of Independence, Du Bois said,

"The black men of America have a duty to perform, a duty stern and delicate, –a forward movement to oppose a part of the work of their greatest leader. So far as Mr. Washington preaches Thrift, Patience, and Industrial Training for the masses, we must hold up his hands and strive with him, rejoicing in his honors and glorying in the strength of this Joshua called of God and of man to lead the headless host. But so far as Mr. Washington apologizes for injustice, North or South, does not rightly value the privilege and duty of voting, belittles the emasculating effects of caste distinctions, and opposes the higher training and ambitions of our brighter minds, –so far as he, the South, or the Nation, does this, –we must unceasingly and firmly oppose them. By every civilized and peaceful method we must strive for the rights which the world accords to men, clinging unwaveringly to those great words which the sons of the Fathers would fain forget: 'We hold these truths to be self-evident: That all men are created equal; that they are endowed by their Creator with certain unalienable rights; that among these are life, liberty, and the pursuit of happiness."[12]

W.E.B. Du Bois

Deeper Roots
Eugenics

Despite Du Bois's striving for equality, his generation remained trapped as second-tier citizens, with enormous new roadblocks to racial integration being constructed. One of the largest was an emerging scientific field called *eugenics*. Just a few decades prior, the theory of natural selection had been introduced by Charles Darwin. His basic idea was that humans evolve through a series of very small changes, whereby useless changes die out and useful changes are passed to subsequent generations. Soon thereafter, Darwin's cousin, Francis Galton, founded eugenics, a study of artificial interventions to speed the natural process of evolution. Galton believed humans could be improved by isolating and breeding people with the greatest "genetic worth."

Lacking any legitimate measure of genetic worth, scientists crudely used occupation and social class as a proxy. Independent professionals, large employers, skilled workmen, and clerks were assumed to have superior genetics. Conversely, the financially poor, criminals, and other undesirables were viewed as genetic inferiors.[13] And there was an obvious link between perceptions of genetic worth and views on race. Poverty among minorities, despite its connection to a long history of injustice, was assumed to result from inferior genetics.

As outlandish as it may seem today, eugenics gained popular acceptance in the early 1900s. A Station for Experimental Evolution was established for breeding experiments, with funding from Andrew Carnegie. A Eugenics Record Office was created to collect biological and social information about the US population. And when the International Federation of Eugenics Organization was founded, a US citizen served as its first president. Not coincidentally, the 1920s became the all-time peak of membership for the Ku Klux Klan.

As Du Bois and others continued fighting for racial equity, an even larger fight was brewing around the world. Many nations aggressively sought territorial expansion, and they were bound to encroach on one another's domain. From the late 1800s through the early 1900s, Europeans scrambled for control of Africa, much like they had scrambled for the Americas several centuries prior. More than 95% of African land was overtaken by European empires.[14] Europeans also gained control across much of Asia.[c]

With lands being forcefully taken, armed conflict was inevitable, and the battles quickly spread across the globe. Today, the years 1914 to 1918 are remembered as World War I, the world's first global fight. Beginning as a European war, it pulled in other nations through alliances. The United States entered late and emerged triumphant, but much of the nation regretted its involvement. The costs of war were severe—more than one hundred thousand US deaths—and for what? In the minds of many US leaders, victory had delivered no obvious

c. During this same era, the United States gained control of vulnerable island nations. The Philippines, a collection of islands to the southeast of China, became property of the United States for nearly fifty years. Several territories closer to mainland United States were also acquired and remain part of the nation to this day: Hawaii, Puerto Rico, Guam, and the US Virgin Islands. The United States occupied several other countries for shorter periods of time, including Cuba, Haiti, the Dominican Republic, and Nicaragua.

gains. So the nation disengaged from the war's aftermath in Europe and committed to a new policy of isolationism.

One way Congress secluded the nation was enacting its firmest ever immigration restrictions, called the *national origins quota system*, in the early 1920s. Under this new law, many countries in the world were assigned annual quotas, capping their number of immigrants to the United States, and the quotas varied greatly by country. The largest, by far, went to countries in Northwest Europe. They were favored, explicitly and openly. According to the US Department of State, the quota system aimed "to preserve the ideal of US homogeneity."[15]

With these new immigration restrictions in place and World War I in the rear-view mirror, the four largest racial and ethnic groups faced very different situations in 1930.

The **Black** population represented 10% of the nation, and they were on the move. This era was the first of two phases of what would become known as the Great Migration, a mass exodus of Black people out of the South. Since the nation's founding, at least nine out of every ten Black people had resided in Southern states.[d] In the early 1900s, for the first time ever, they were finding opportunities elsewhere. Millions headed north and, to a lesser extent, west, for varied reasons. For one, they could enjoy greater freedoms in states where Jim Crow laws were less strict. They also sought greater security. Though lynching activity was down from its 1890s peak, it was still common, and lynching was most prevalent in the South. Perhaps even more impactful, there were job opportunities for Black people outside of the South. With the nation industrializing, and immigrant numbers down, urban factories needed workers.

Another people group needed for their labor was the **Hispanic**[e] population, most of whom traced ancestry to Mexico. This era

---

d. Here, "South" conforms to the current US Census Bureau definition, which expands beyond the bounds of the former Confederacy. It includes sixteen states plus Washington DC.
e. The term "Hispanic" was not common in the early 1900s. Here, Hispanic refers to people who would likely identify today as Hispanic or Latino.

marked the beginning of a century-long movement of people from Mexico to the United States. Initially, they were welcomed here. In fact, when quotas restricted the number of immigrants arriving from most countries, no limits were placed on Mexican immigrants. They were invited to walk through open doors. Companies in the United States recruited Mexican newcomers, taking advantage of their less-expensive labor, as the US economy roared through the 1920s. As a portion of total new immigrants, Hispanic people rose from 2% in the first decade of the 1900s to 14% in the 1920s. In total, though, the Hispanic population was relatively small. Still not separately counted in the census, they comprised 1%–2% of the nation as of 1930.[f,16]

Even smaller, rounding down to 0% of all US residents, was the **Asian** population, and Congress aimed to keep their number low. As a special provision of the new immigration restrictions, no quota was assigned to Asian immigrants. They were banned. Congress extended Chinese Exclusion to all of Asia, adopting the view espoused by California voters several decades prior: persons ruled ineligible for citizenship were not even allowed to enter the country. Even newcomers from Japan, a World War I ally and key trading partner of the United States, were turned away.

Lastly, the **White** majority was numerically dominant, more so than it ever had been. As of the nation's first census, in 1790, about 80% of residents had been White. Thereafter, with European immigrants arriving at the East Coast and Asian immigrants being turned away at the West Coast, the White majority had increased, reaching about 89% by 1930.

And the perimeter around the inner circle of White leadership had become nearly impenetrable. Every single one of the more than three thousand Congressional seats filled between 1901 and 1928 went to a White person.[17] Even as the nation extended voting rights to women, electing twenty-two women to Congress in the 1920s

---

f. In 1930, and in that year alone, *Mexican* was included in the Census as a race.

alone, the democratic voice of racial minorities was kept silent. Congress operated as a Whites-only club. And when a Black man was finally elected in 1929, breaking the long drought of minority representation, the poem "Niggers in the White House" resurfaced. It was even read in a session of Congress.[18]

The era thus ended much as it had begun. Racial bias was entrenching, the White majority was strengthening, and the economy was surging. None of those trends, however, would continue much longer.

Deeper Roots
Progress and Prejudice

Setting aside differences by race and ethnicity, the early 1900s was another era of economic progress. The exhilaration of railroads was surpassed by the introduction of personal automobiles. National infrastructure also improved, with telephone lines and electricity extending into homes and changing daily patterns of life. And there was a flood of new labor-saving innovations, such as washing machines and vacuum cleaners.

Along with the majority White population, minorities benefitted from such economic progress. Between 1900 and 1930, their childhood school enrollment leapt from 44% to 84%, and adult literacy climbed from 51% to 83%. Average life expectancy for minorities greatly improved, too, up from a paltry thirty-three years to forty-six years.

Despite those gains, though, minorities were still relegated to lower positions in both capitalism and democracy. They were often only considered for the less desirable jobs and not trained for the better paying positions. Differences by occupation were captured in census results. As of 1930, 70% of minority workers were still general laborers or service workers, versus only 31% of White workers. Differences by race were particularly noticeable amongst private household servants. They represented 17% of the entire minority workforce and only 2% of the White workforce. The opposite was true of higher-paying occupations. Positions in sales, public service, professional services, and clerical services were seldom filled by minorities.[19]

Minorities continued advancing, yet they remained far behind.[20]

	Minority[g]			White[h]		
	1870	1900	1930	1870	1900	1930
Percent of US population	13%	12%	11%	87%	88%	89%
Percent of US Congress	1%	0%	0%	99%	100%	100%
School enrollment, ages 7–15	13%	44%	84%	67%	74%	93%
Adult literacy, age 15+	19%	51%	83%	88%	93%	97%
Life expectancy at birth	NA	33	46	NA	48	61
Labor force in agriculture	71%	57%	38%	48%	35%	20%

g. Minority encompasses all races other than White. The relatively small Hispanic population was included within White. The 1870 Census included Black, Mulatto, (American) Indian, and Chinese, and the 1900 Census added Japanese. In all three census years shown, more than nine out of every ten minorities were identified as Black or Mulatto.
h. Non-Hispanic White

Minority representation in Congress returned to 0%.[i,21]

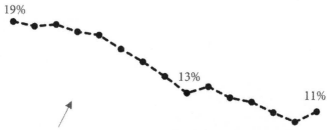

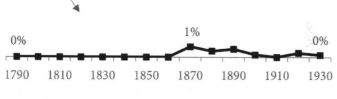

As a portion of the nation's population, minorities steadily declined.
As a portion of Congress, minorities remained close to 0%.

■ Minority % of Congress ⬤ Minority % of the population

---

i. Chart only shows data points for decennial years. Minority representation peaked at 2% in 1875, which does not appear on the chart.

CHAPTER 8

Segregating Threats (1930–1950)

THE US ECONOMY roared through the 1920s, blinding wealthy investors with excitement. Eager to obtain financial rewards, they lost sight of financial risks. Overconfidence pushed stock market prices well above reasonable values and created a recipe for disaster. After rising nearly 500% from 1921 to 1929, stock markets were bound to fall. But nobody could have anticipated the speed and depths of that fall.

Just a couple months before the calendar turned to 1930, tides of optimism gave way to a current of doubt, and the stock market receded. The surprise of market losses shook confidence, causing consumer spending and investment activity to fall. Stocks dipped further in response. Struggling businesses fired some employees and cut wages for others. Stocks dipped further still. Cash-strapped bank customers demanded their savings, and banks could not come up with cash quickly enough. Banks failed, and stock values reached new lows.

Over three years, nearly 90% of wealth held in US stock markets disappeared.[1] Investors lost their 1920s gains plus quite a bit more. It was the start of the Great Depression, still regarded as the worst economic period in US history. By 1933, nearly half of the nation's banks had failed. Economic euphoria had turned into panic and distress.

Across the nation, people were pushed to extraordinary means to survive, and minorities were especially vulnerable. At the time, there were no federal laws prohibiting hiring or firing based on race alone. When financial stress forced business owners into difficult employment decisions, minority workers were often the last to be hired and the first to be fired.

Government leaders hotly debated the underlying causes of the economic downturn. One commonly cited factor was the imbalance of wealth and income across the population. Financial prosperity had become concentrated in too few hands, with half of all income going to just 10% of the population. A quarter of all income went to the top 1%.[2] Such extreme imbalance was unsettling. It meant some people could dismiss the Great Depression as a pest soon to fly away, while others battled it as a predator threatening death by starvation.

～

I found such extreme inequalities in my own family, and they disturbed me. John Chesney's descendants were living comfortably in the 1930s, while Pharaoh's descendants faced extreme challenges. And their vastly different fortunes could be linked to past injustices. By this point in my journey, I had made peace with my slave-owning ancestors, who felt far removed, but now my studies were getting more personal.

Warren Chesney, great-grandson of John Chesney, was born in 1914. Warren was my grandfather, a man I dearly loved. I will never forget the years of visiting his bedside table in a nursing home. A misfit in that facility, he kept a bright mind until his final breath. Lou Gehrig's disease paralyzed him, shoulders down, while leaving everything above intact. And he had far more than just intellect. If there ever was a Boy Scout, it was he. He was a card-carrying member, literally, and he saved those cards long enough to pass to me. They sit on my desk at home, alongside his Troop Seventeen badge and Boy Scout diaries. Warren's membership cards include the Scout Law, which begins with a pledge to be trustworthy, loyal, helpful, and friendly. Those words describe my experience of my grandfather.

He was also a person granted privileges from an early age. I only recently recognized them and considered the impact they had on his life and, therefore, mine. Without certain privileges, I do not believe my grandfather would have earned the prosperity and esteem that came in adulthood. He encountered several major trials, and each time he was given a soft landing.

Warren's life started with tragedy, losing his father at age three. His mother, suddenly a single parent with no income, could have spiraled into a life of poverty. But they were saved by Warren's uncle, his mother's brother. An established physician, Warren's uncle cared for Warren as his own child.

When the Great Depression came, many kids in Warren's generation had their lives upended. But not Warren. Prosperity in his new home shielded him from the risks of poverty. Warren's Boy Scout diaries gave me an inside view of his childhood. I only have two of them, but they happen to be from the first two years of the Great Depression. At ages fourteen and fifteen, my grandfather recorded events from every single day, without exception. His entries tell stories of carefree fun, not of struggle. There were school events, library trips, Tennessee football games, ping-pong matches, family hikes, and downtown shows. At the lowest point of the depression, he was even afforded the tremendous privilege of a college education—in his era, only 6% of White kids and 2% of Black kids could go to college.[3] And Warren did not stop there. As the Great Depression continued, he graduated college and entered medical school, progressing smoothly along an expensive path to lifetime prosperity.

Meanwhile, Paul Henry Chesney, great-grandson of Pharaoh, was living separate and unequal. He resided only a few miles down the road from Warren, as he had for their entire lives. I doubt either of them knew of the other's existence. Apart from proximity, their lives were nothing alike.

Like most other Black families, Paul's was financially poor. Despite living in poverty with illiterate parents, Paul still learned to read, but he only stayed in school through the fourth grade. That was common. Nationally, only 12% of Black kids completed high school, compared to 41% of White kids.[4] While Warren sat in classrooms, Paul toiled in fields to help support his family. He worked side-by-side with his father, seventy-eight hours per week, fifty-two weeks per year.[5] For families like his, the Great Depression was a fight for survival.

Extreme financial inequalities, such as those between Warren and Paul, were not lost on Congress. Hoping to ease daily struggles faced by people with low incomes, Congress entertained major economic reforms. One of the most prominent was the Share Our Wealth program, proposed by a flamboyant US senator, Huey Long. Aiming to more broadly spread wealth, his revolutionary plan called for capping the size of personal fortunes and redistributing excesses to the general population.

Senator Long drummed up support for his plan by appealing to the public's frustration with the wealthiest of the wealthy. He even called out individuals by name in a speech to Congress, saying,

> "How many men ever went to a barbecue and would let one man take off the table what's intended for nine tenths of the people to eat? The only way you'll ever be able to feed the balance of the people is to make that man come back and bring back some of that grub he ain't got no business with...What's Morgan and Baruch and Rockefeller and Mellon going to do with all of that grub? They can't eat it. They can't wear the clothes. They can't live in the houses. Give 'em a yacht! Give 'em a palace! Send them

to Reno and get them a new wife when they want it, if that's what they want. But when they've got everything on the God's loving earth that they can eat and they can wear and they can live in, and all that their children can live in and wear and eat, and all their children's children can use, then we got to call Mr. Morgan and Mr. Mellon and Mr. Rockefeller back and say, 'Come back here. Put that stuff back on this table here that you took away from here—that you don't need. Leave something else for the American people to consume.' And that's the program."[6]

Senator Huey Long

There was a groundswell of backing for the Share Our Wealth program. Proponents formed support clubs across the nation, with membership surpassing seven million.[7] Ultimately, their most progressive proposals would fizzle, but they softened the public to other bold ideas. Under the leadership of President Franklin D. Roosevelt and First Lady Eleanor Roosevelt, Congress passed a bevy of landmark acts. Together, they were branded as the New Deal, promising to kick-start the economy and make it fairer for average people. This was by far the largest ever, federal intervention in the economy.

Franklin D. Roosevelt

Relief provided by New Deal programs extended to all racial groups. Some legislation contained provisions prohibiting racial discrimination, and the White House even included Black leaders among its advisors. Yet the New Deal also had an ugly side. Some new federal programs conformed to prevailing sentiment about race, staining their long-term legacy. Those in power lacked the resolve or foresight to set the nation on a path leading to racial integration. Instead, they often worsened segregation while disproportionately delivering assistance to the majority White population.

A prime example came in federal intervention in the housing industry, which aimed to solve housing shortages and boost related businesses. At the time, renting homes was more common than owning homes because typical home mortgages were prohibitively expensive, requiring a 50% down payment and a payback period of five years or less.[8] Many people simply could not afford those terms. So the government tried to help.

Federal intervention in the housing industry centered on mortgage subsidies, provided through a partnership between the Federal Housing Administration (FHA) and private banks. In effect, the government agreed to accept some risk of mortgage defaults in exchange for banks lowering the cost of mortgages. The arrangement had many winners. Banks reaped financial rewards and created jobs as their business volumes grew. Construction companies and their suppliers did the same. And many homeowners received lower monthly mortgage payments.

All in all, the program was a huge success; home ownership rates skyrocketed and have not since fallen back. But there would also be long-term, negative consequences because mortgage subsidies were restricted to segregated neighborhoods. The government would not help minorities if they tried to enter majority White neighborhoods, and banks steered clear of minority neighborhoods because they viewed them as high risk.

Racial bias was at the root of this discrimination. The government believed the very presence of minorities in White neighborhoods would render homes undesirable. As a result, home values could sink below outstanding mortgage balances, causing White homeowners to default, and taxpayers could be left paying the bill. In the government's mind, the way to avoid such losses was to remove the "threat" of integration. Instead of addressing the root problem, racial bias, the government kicked the costs of bias down the road for future generations to pay.

Deeper Roots
Residential Segregation and the Federal Housing Administration

The federal government's role in promoting residential segregation was captured in official records. The Federal Housing Administration's (FHA) 1936 underwriting manual said,

"The Valuator should investigate areas surrounding the location to determine whether or not incompatible racial and social groups are present, to the end that an intelligent prediction may be made regarding the possibility or probability of the location being invaded by such groups. If a neighborhood is to retain stability it is necessary that properties shall continue to be occupied by the same social and racial classes. A change in social or racial occupancy generally leads to instability and a reduction in values. The protection offered against adverse changes should be found adequate before a high rating is given to this feature."[9]

Federal Housing Administration

The federal government did not stop there. Homeowners in segregated neighborhoods could even be rejected due to the mere possibility of future integration. Clear lines of defense protecting segregation were required, the most effective being restrictive covenants, such as private deed restrictions. They were written contracts that could equally restrict the color of paint outside a house and the color of people inside a house. If every house in a White neighborhood was bound by restrictive covenants, then homeowners could rest easy knowing racial minorities would be kept away.

The federal government was not a direct party in private contracts, but it empowered them. Deed restrictions were upheld by the Supreme Court[a], imposed by local law enforcement, and promoted by the FHA, whose underwriting manual advised, "Recorded deed restrictions should strengthen and supplement zoning ordinances. Recommended restrictions include . . . prohibition of the occupancy of properties except by the race for which they are intended."[10]

a. Corrigan v. Buckley, (1926)

Sometimes, even deed restrictions were deemed insufficient to resist the threat of integration. Multiple lines of defense, including physical barriers, were required. The government wanted to see a residential map with literal lines dividing racial groups: White on one side, minority on the other, and no mixing allowed. Physical barriers could be natural, like a river, or unnatural, like a highway or concrete wall.

"Where little or no protection is provided against adverse influences the Valuator must not hesitate to make a reject rating of this feature . . . Natural or artificially established barriers will prove effective in protecting a neighborhood and the locations within it from adverse influences. Usually the protection against adverse influences afforded by these means include prevention of the infiltration of business and industrial uses, lower class occupancy, and inharmonious racial groups."[11]

Federal Housing Administration

There would be other costs, too, because forced segregation was just one of many stains on New Deal programs. Discrimination also came in the form of occupational restrictions that limited who could receive federal benefits. Most notably, all agricultural and domestic workers were ruled ineligible, and they alone accounted for 65% of Black workers and only 27% of White workers.[12]

When Social Security was launched in 1935, occupational restrictions applied. Agricultural and domestic workers were disqualified from receiving the cash assistance provided by Social Security.[b] Occupational restrictions also applied to worker protections.

Congress also set the first-ever minimum wage at twenty-five cents per hour, mandated higher pay for work weeks exceeding forty hours, and defended the right of workers to unionize. While those regulations were celebrated by people in included occupations, agricultural laborers and domestic workers were again excluded.

Some people cite racial bias as the reason for occupational restrictions in New Deal programs. Others point to administrative challenges, noting it would have been infeasible to monitor millions of small farms and residences. I suspect the truth is somewhere in between. Regardless of the causes, the effect was the same. Most Black workers were excluded, while most White workers were included. Federal benefits did not address the heightened vulnerability of minority populations, and federal intervention sometimes pushed racial groups people further apart.

And there are even more roots of racial division buried in this era. Tragically, it was a time when some racial groups were outright

---

b. Agricultural and domestic workers were glad to also be exempt from paying associated payroll taxes, but they would have been better served by paying the taxes and receiving the benefits because the first generation of Social Security recipients received guaranteed lifetime income despite paying little into the system.

attacked, inflicting financial and emotional wounds that still fester today. Hispanic and Asian people had to overcome far more than just income imbalance and New Deal discriminations. Each group was regarded as a threat to be removed or contained.

For Hispanic people, the attack came in the form of forced expulsion. They were no longer wanted in the country, even if they were US-born citizens, and even if their ancestors were the original inhabitants of America. Though Hispanic people had been officially counted as White, they were always treated as a lesser type of White. It was as if they had been allowed to enter the nation's inner circle only to sit in chairs around the perimeter. In the center of the circle were "true Whites," those who traced their ancestry only to Europe. When the economy collapsed, the true Whites felt threatened by people sitting at the perimeter of the circle. So the true Whites ganged up on them and physically threw them out of the room. And not just newcomers. The true Whites threw out lifelong members, too. According to Californian legislators,

> "In total, it is estimated that two million people of Mexican ancestry were forcibly relocated to Mexico, approximately 1.2 million of whom had been born in the United States, including the State of California. Throughout California, massive raids were conducted on Mexican-American communities, resulting in the clandestine removal of thousands of people, many of whom were never able to return to the United States, their country of birth. These raids also had the effect of coercing thousands of people to leave the country in the face of threats and acts of violence. These raids targeted persons of Mexican ancestry, with authorities and others indiscriminately characterizing these persons as 'illegal

aliens' even when they were United States citizens or permanent legal residents."[c,13]

State of California

Shortly thereafter, people of Japanese origin were similarly targeted. They were not thrown out of the room, like Hispanic people. Instead, they were essentially locked in a closet—an act of war motivated by fear and perpetrated by their own country, the United States.

This travesty occurred soon after imperial ambitions had spawned another global fight. This time it was World War II. As with World War I, much of the US public hoped to stay out of the fight, but attitudes quickly changed in 1941. That was when Japan, an ally of Germany, surprise attacked Pearl Harbor on the Hawaiian Islands. Compelled to respond, the US government rapidly organized a large armed force. Adult men of every race were required to register for a war draft, a lottery with an unenviable prize. Among the millions drafted into service, there were about thirty-three thousand US residents of Japanese ancestry, most of who were sent into battle in Europe. Tragically, while they fought overseas for their home country, the United States, their families were treated as enemies. Blinded by fear, the federal government treated all people of Japanese ancestry as one undesirable group.

Federal investigators sought evidence to confirm fears that people of Japanese ancestry were sabotaging the nation, and not even one instance was found. Nevertheless, President Roosevelt ordered all of them to be forcefully removed from the West Coast and incarcerated in camps in the nation's interior. More than one hundred thousand were held captive, most of them US citizens

---

c. Quotation is taken from an official statement by the State of California in 2005. Estimates of the number of people forcibly relocated to Mexico widely vary. Some suggest the number was far lower than two million. People relocated for a variety of reasons, and it is difficult to separate the impact of racial bias and coercion from that of other considerations, such as unemployment in the United States and desire to return to family members in Mexico.

by birth. Their captivity was controversial from the beginning. Letters sent to army offices protested the idea of incarcerating families while their sons served US interests overseas, but the protests proved futile. The general in charge of defending the West Coast convinced Congress to stand firm, declaring,

> "I don't want any of them here. They are a dangerous element. There is no way to determine their loyalty . . . The danger of the Japanese was, and is now,—if they are permitted to come back—espionage and sabotage. It makes no difference whether he is an American citizen, he is still a Japanese."[14]
>
> *General John DeWitt*

Racial bias was an obvious factor in their incarceration. People of Japanese ancestry were a small minority of the US population, and US leaders associated them with a World War II enemy nation, Japan. But Japan was not the only wartime enemy. The ultimate aggressor was Germany, and there were far more people of German ancestry living in the United States. As White citizens, German Americans maintained their freedoms, while Japanese Americans were incarcerated. In hindsight, the double standard is obvious. Several decades later, as part of an official apology, Congress would admit,

> ". . . a grave injustice was done to both citizens and permanent resident aliens of Japanese ancestry by the evacuation, relocation, and internment of civilians during World War II. As the Commission documents, these actions were carried out without adequate security reasons and without any acts of espionage or sabotage documented by the Commission, and were motivated largely by racial prejudice, wartime hysteria, and a failure of political leadership. The excluded individuals

of Japanese ancestry suffered enormous damages, both material and intangible, and there were incalculable losses in education and job training, all of which resulted in significant human suffering . . ."[15]

US Congress

The injustices of this era were too great for me to digest. From New Deal discriminations to the removal of Mexican Americans to Japanese incarceration, the events were so shocking that they felt abstract, disconnected from real people. In my head, I knew the effects were deeply personal, but I needed to see a tangible example. So I looked back to my own family.

When World War II began, Warren, my grandfather, had just started his medical practice. Like so many other young men, his life took a detour, as he was drafted into the armed forces and sent into battle in Europe. When he returned home, though, he found yet another soft landing. Benefitting from a medical degree and family wealth, Warren constructed a forty-seven-hundred-square-foot suburban home across from the country club. There, his family settled down—living comfortably in a large home, surrounded by others like them, and having benefitted from countless privileges and protections. That is the life my father was born into and the house in which he was raised.

Most soldiers, of course, returned to less fortunate circumstances, and the government wanted to lend them a hand. So Congress enacted a Servicemen's Readjustment Act, also known as the G.I. Bill, providing a range of benefits to returning servicemen. It included major subsidies for home mortgages and college education. But these benefits were beyond reach for some servicemen. Like the Federal Housing Administration, the Veterans Administration guaranteed mortgages on a racially discriminatory basis. Furthermore, taking advantage of a subsidized education and mortgage required first being accepted by a college and approved for a loan by a bank.

Racial bias was a huge barrier in both cases. And even with subsidies, the cost of education and homes was greater than most Black servicemen could afford. In short, the G.I. bill was not tailored to address unique challenges faced by racial minorities, who returned home to lives characterized by obstacles, not privileges.

For instance, consider Paul Chesney's experience. Like Warren, Paul was drafted into service during World War II and fought overseas. After the war, Paul resumed working in the same fields where he had worked before the war. As compensation, he received just seven cents per hour, a low wage even in that era.[16] I do not know the extent to which racial bias influenced his meager pay. Economic forces of supply and demand may have determined his wage, but New Deal minimum wages superseded those forces for people in other occupations. As an agricultural laborer, Paul was among the millions excluded from worker protections. He worked nearly twice the forty-hour-work-week standard for compensation of less than a third of the twenty-five-cent minimum wage.

Working the fields, Paul could at least afford the ten-dollar monthly rent for his home, the same home in which he had lived before the war. There, his family settled down—making ends meet in a small, rented home, having overcome many obstacles.

Taking a step back, I realized Paul, descendant of an enslaved, and my grandfather, descendant of an enslaver, were born on diverging paths and progressed along them predictably. They achieved very different financial outcomes, which meant their kids were provided very different opportunities. Before long, similar differences would extend to their grandkids, which includes me. Like I said before, my studies were starting to get too close for comfort.

∾

Approaching the year 1950, I was about to turn a critical corner in my walk through the story of race. Not only was I creeping toward my life, but I was also entering the years known as the *civil rights era.* That was the time when racial equity had finally been achieved, or so I was told in sixth grade. I was anxious to look back upon the civil rights era with fresh eyes. First, though, I needed to pause and recalibrate. I felt disoriented, my mind spinning from everything I had already learned. So I briefly reviewed my learning and took stock of life in America at the mid-point of the 1900s, when my parents were born.

To start, I considered the good, and there was plenty. Unlike many other countries of the era, the United States had advanced personal liberties. Under democracy, the most powerful leaders could be openly opposed, and no small group or dictator could overpower the general population. Even more impressive was the capitalist economy. The nation had fully rebounded from the Great Depression and picked up where it let off, with impressive advances in quality of life. In the first half of the 1900s, life expectancy increased by more than twenty years in the United States; not just for White people, but also for minorities.[17] Over the same time period, the infant mortality rate fell by more than two-thirds. Education seemed to soar as well. Childhood school enrollment rates rose above 70% for both the majority White population and minorities. And illiteracy rates improved, declining from 6% to 2% for White adults, and plunging from 44% to 11% for minorities.[18] On the surface, there was much to be applauded.

Underneath, though, racial injustice was still deeply rooted. **Socially**, people in the United States were strictly separated by race, and they always had been. There was a clear distinction between people classified as White, who were regarded as superior, and all the rest, who were regarded as inferior. The majority White population overpowered all others, restricting their opportunities and freedoms. In a democracy, that was both possible and legal because the majority set the rules.

Racial minorities were banned from participating as equals. They were continuously excluded, treated as lepers, with a contagious disease. They could not go to certain shows. Could not take their kids to the best city parks. Could not enter most public libraries. Could not serve on juries. Could not drink from the cleanest water fountains. Could not eat at the best restaurants. Could not sit in certain seating sections. Could not marry whomever they loved. In short, they were not yet fully free.

Shifting my focus from social issues to the **financial**, I again noted the enormous inequality. It was allowed, perhaps even required, by capitalism. Inequality may have been foundational to the success of capitalism, but it seemed to come at a great cost. There was high potential for financial failure, with a strong correlation to racial identity. Typical minority families received only about half as much income as typical White families.[19] And the gap in wealth was even greater.

The cause of those gaps was obvious. After centuries enslaving others, the White majority had only agreed to liberty for all over their own literal dead bodies, as the bitter outcome of Civil War. And freedom came along with nothing else: no reparations, no apologies. The majority population had begrudgingly made citizens of freed people and then written new rules ensuring total racial separation. In short, minorities had started from behind and been kept there.

Furthermore, the center point of capitalism, free markets, was largely a sham. US markets were not free; they were clearly encumbered by racial bias. The White majority did not allow minorities to compete as equals. As prospective employees, they were not fairly considered for jobs. As business owners, they struggled to secure seed capital from White bank managers, to sell to White customers, or to form partnerships with White businesses owners.

Lastly, I considered **democratic representation**. The White majority still controlled the nation with an iron fist. Out of 502 people in Congress in 1950, there were only four minorities. All the rest were White and non-Hispanic.

As a nearly 100% White body, Congress exercised its legislative authority to protect White control. Intimidation, literacy tests, and poll taxes still turned away minority voters. And immigration and citizenship were still restricted based on race, with Asians almost entirely banned.

∿

These many concerns about the underbelly of America weighed me down as I turned the page to the civil rights era. I was worried democracy at its worst could be unrestricted individual liberty—majority rule upholding majority beliefs, without regard for minority concerns. As for capitalism, it seemed to run on the fuel of self-interest. Unfettered, it could create a world where relatively few winners take all and keep all. In short, the US model could deliver great benefits to a powerful majority, while exacting great costs from a weaker minority.

Deeper Roots
Signs of Coming Change

By the end of World War II, factories had been remobilized and the nation set back on a course of growth. Industries regained their stride, sending unemployment down and stock markets up. The rebound was so strong that the US economy found itself more powerful than ever before.

Soothed by victory and prosperity, some White leaders softened their defense against integration. In 1947, Major League Baseball became the first professional sport to include a Black player, allowing Jackie Robinson to join its top league. His immediate performance on the field left no doubt that Black players had been excluded due to their race, not their ability. In

Robinson's first season, he earned Rookie of the Year honors. Two years later, he led the league in hitting and steals, earning the Most Valuable Player award.

Not to be outdone by baseball, the Supreme Court also reversed course. In 1948, the Court decided it would no longer enforce restrictive covenants, contracts preventing racial minorities from purchasing or renting homes in many residential areas. Private citizens would still be allowed to racially discriminate in housing, but the court would no longer enforce such written agreements.[20]

A few months later, White House leaders softened as well. On the heels of a war in which US battle units were segregated by race, President Harry Truman directed armed forces down a path toward racial equity. He signed an executive order calling for the integration of US armed forces, further commanding, "There shall be equality of treatment and opportunity for all persons in the armed forces without regard to race, color, religion, or national origin."[21]

CHAPTER 9

Conceding Civility (1950–1970)

OVER THE NEXT two decades, from 1950 to 1970, the attention of US leaders would be divided between two battlefronts. Abroad, communism was surging, and the United States was committed to containing its spread. Meanwhile, at home, racial minorities were demanding greater freedoms, prompting stiff resistance from the White majority. Those simultaneous fights would become inextricably linked.

As for the fight against communism, its primary battleground was in Asia. By 1950, China had chosen communism, Vietnam was strongly leaning in that direction, and Korea was split between communism and democracy. The world's two leading superpowers, the United States and the Soviet Union, each sent troops to Asia to advance their respective ideologies, the United States fighting for democracy and the Soviet Union for communism. War had engulfed Korea, and a similar fight was brewing in Vietnam.

The United States did not engage in these battles hoping to gain territory. More elusive, the ultimate objective was shaping mindsets. Eventually, US forces would withdraw and allow Asian people to make and defend their own choices, and when that time came, US leaders hoped Asian people would choose democracy of their own free will. Thus, victory required proving the US way of governance was superior to communism.

In this ideological war, the United States faced a huge credibility problem due to its treatment of racial minorities. For the first time in human history, technology was enabling news reports to spread globally in near real time. Racial injustice was impossible to hide. Some international media made it seem as if the United States had stepped onto the world's stage with its pants down—naked and uncomfortable, flaws fully exposed. The Soviet Union, more than any other country, weaponized US faults to brand the country as an oppressor rather than a beacon of liberty. US leaders were called hypocrites. While appealing for democratic freedoms abroad, they were criticized for limiting civil rights in their own country. President Truman's Committee on Civil Rights warned,

> "Our civil rights record has growing international implications . . . The pervasive gap between our aims and what we actually do is creating a kind of moral dry rot which eats away at the emotional and rational bases of democratic beliefs. There are times when the difference between what we preach about civil rights and what we practice is shockingly illustrated by individual outrages. There are times when the whole structure of our ideology is made ridiculous by individual instances. And there are certain continuing, quiet, omnipresent practices which do irreparable damage to our beliefs . . . We cannot escape the fact that our civil rights record has been an issue in world politics. The world's press and radio are full of it . . . They have tried to prove our democracy an empty fraud, and our nation a consistent oppressor of underprivileged people."[1]
>
> *Truman's Committee on Civil Rights*

President Truman and other key leaders correctly assessed the situation. The only surefire way to overcome Soviet propaganda was to strip it of truth. Like it or not, shaping mindsets abroad required accepting change at home. From the outside looking in, the United States needed to appear as a worthy role model for other nations.

A huge step toward this end came in 1954, with a Supreme Court ruling in the field of education. Over the preceding decades, lawyers for the National Association for the Advancement of Colored People (NAACP) had won cases appealing educational equality, but isolated wins had not changed the overall trajectory of education. Public schools were still separated by race, and White students were given superior opportunities to succeed. So the NAACP decided on a more comprehensive strategy. They would challenge the very notion of "separate but equal," insisting forced separation inherently created inequality. After four years aggressively arguing their case, the NAACP finally won the Supreme Court's support. Issuing a shocking repudiation of segregated schooling, the justices unanimously declared,

> "Does segregation of children in public schools solely on the basis of race, even though the physical facilities and other 'tangible' factors may be equal, deprive the children of the minority group of equal educational opportunities? We believe that it does . . . Such considerations apply with added force to children in grade and high schools. To separate them from others of similar age and qualifications solely because of their race generates a feeling of inferiority as to their status in the community that may affect their hearts and minds in a way unlikely ever to be undone . . . We conclude that in the field of public education the doctrine of 'separate but equal' has no place. Separate educational facilities are inherently unequal."[2]
>
> *Supreme Court majority opinion*

The Court's message was clear; no longer could states racially segregate public education. And though the ruling had no immediate impact outside of education, many people believed there would be a domino effect. If schools were to be integrated, then perhaps similar transformation would happen in other major spheres of society. Winds of change were clearly blowing the nation away from racial discrimination and toward inclusion.

Every step in that direction, however, would be met with heavy White resistance. Notably, not all White people clung to the status quo. Some of them, and then many, and later most, either genuinely wanted progress toward racial equity or conceded it was necessary to win the fight against communism. But if the winds of change had to blow, most White leaders wanted a gentle breeze toward a destination still under White control. There was no appetite for a storm of revolutionary force. So whenever they sensed a potential loss of power, they resisted.

White families feeling threatened by the idea of integrated schooling leapt into action, calling on elected officials to protect their children. More than one hundred members of Congress, including the entire delegations of seven Southern states, signed a protest entitled "The Southern Manifesto." Their joint statement insisted racial segregation was a state right and characterized the Supreme Court's ruling as an abuse of judicial power. The manifesto closed with a pledge to resist enforcement, and it was not an empty promise. The Southern Manifesto's bark had a vicious bite.

When nine Black kids registered for an all-White high school in Little Rock, Arkansas, Governor Orval Faubus objected and ordered state troops to block the school's entrance. The kids bravely arrived for the first day of school, and ugly scenes followed. Before being turned away by armed guards, they were harassed by several hundred protesters. Some screamed racial slurs and threatened death by lynching. Sensing danger, one of the kids, a fifteen-year old girl, recalled her futile search for an ally.

"They glared at me with a mean look and I was very frightened and didn't know what to do. I turned around and the crowd came toward me. Somebody started yelling, 'Lynch her! Lynch her!' I tried to see a friendly face somewhere in the mob, someone who maybe would help. I looked into the face of an old woman and it seemed a kind face, but when I looked at her again, she spat on me."[3]

Elizabeth Eckford

In a national embarrassment, news cameras captured the ugly scenes and broadcast them around the world. The nation's foremost leader, President Dwight Eisenhower, needed to act, but he had mixed feelings about the proper response. On one hand, he was sympathetic to the White protestors. He had even tried to sway the Supreme Court toward a different ruling, confiding to its chief justice, "These [White parents] are not bad people. All they are concerned about is to see that their sweet little girls are not required to sit in school alongside some big black bucks."[4] On the other hand, President Eisenhower knew he needed to uphold law and order and worried public defiance would hurt US credibility abroad. Ultimately, Eisenhower did decide to enforce the Court's ruling, justifying his decision pragmatically,

Dwight Eisenhower

"At a time when we face grave situations abroad because of the hatred that communism bears towards a system of government based on human rights, it would be difficult to exaggerate the harm that is being done to the prestige and influence and indeed to the safety of our nation and the world. Our enemies are gloating over this incident and using it everywhere to misrepresent our whole nation."[5]

President Dwight Eisenhower

The nine Black kids returned to the all-White school under protection of five hundred federal troops, sent by the president to overtake the governor's forces. The troops succeeded in enforcing law and order, but there was little they could do to change mindsets. Racial bias, deeply embedded over hundreds of years, had no easy fix.

Defiance against school desegregation continued for many years and took on different forms. To avoid mandatory desegregation, Governor Faubus closed all high schools in Little Rock for a year. Other cities took similarly drastic steps. Norfolk, Virginia, for instance, also shut down public schools to prevent White kids from having to learn alongside Black kids.

Public schools across all states were eventually forced to open their doors and desegregate, but it was a slow process. And some families maintained Whites-only education by banding together to form private schools, or they moved across town to neighborhoods zoned for public schools with the least possible minority representation.

～

My mom lived through these tumultuous years. She was born in 1953, just before the Supreme Court ruled against segregated schooling. If her home state, North Carolina, had obeyed court orders, then she never would have attended an all-White school. But, alas, North Carolina dragged its feet.

Mom and her childhood friends attended their town's only public school, which was reserved for White kids. Educational opportunities for minorities were far less convenient. Though there were empty seats in the local school, minorities were not allowed to fill them. Mom vividly remembers sitting on her grandparents' front porch, watching the "colored bus" transport Black kids twenty miles east to another school. The oddity of the situation confused my mom. Nobody ever explained to her the history behind this prejudice, nor called out its injustice.

What was made clear, though, was the rationale for keeping distance from Cherokee Indians, who lived just a few miles down the road on a reservation. While Mom cannot recall much negative talk about the town's Black residents, she cannot forget the contempt for neighboring Cherokee Indians. She was told they were lazy, irresponsible, and dirty. And their inferior status was reinforced by "funny" names.

The school in Mom's town remained entirely White, off limits to both Black and Cherokee kids, until the mid-1960s. By then, more than a decade had passed since the Supreme Court's landmark ruling against segregated public education.

Mom still remembers the day a Black girl joined her seventh-grade class. Patricia arrived with bobby socks on her feet and worry on her face. To ease her entry, she was given a tour of the school, and my mom was chosen to be the tour guide. Mom's memories of that day have faded over time, but one scene is permanently affixed. She and Patricia—two little girls, one White and one Black—entered a cafeteria room full of White kids. Clearly anxious, Patricia did what young girls do; she reached out and grabbed her new friend's hand for support. It was the first time Mom had ever touched Black skin.

Mom's immediate reaction to Patricia's touch was as naïve as it was profound. "Her skin feels just like mine," Mom realized. "Perhaps we are not that different after all." A simple gesture, a hand holding, accomplished in an instant what words struggle to achieve: changing a mindset.

Other White kids had similar awakenings when a Cherokee girl joined Mom's school. By simply being herself, she challenged the

White community's misconceptions about their Cherokee neighbors. Smart, hard-working, beautiful, and athletically gifted, she became a favorite among her high school classmates. She would go on to earn a college degree from the University of Georgia and was even named Miss UGA.

Experiences like these, learning and living in integrated settings, removed bricks from the walls long-separating racial groups in America. But the walls were tall and sturdy, held together by a clinging to the status quo. Behind every brick removed were stories of grit and courage in the struggle for civil rights.

In the mid-1950s, two Black men stepped to the front lines of this movement. They were Martin Luther King Jr. and Malcolm X. Both men denounced racial segregation and widespread poverty in a land of plenty. Yet they led two distinct movements and often disagreed with one another.

Raised in the South, Martin Luther King Jr. had been forced to abide by rules of racial segregation, and he developed intense disdain for the prevailing system. A college-educated Christian preacher, he regularly intertwined messages about race and politics with proclamations about Jesus, insisting,

Martin Luther King, Jr.

> "The great tragedy is that Christianity failed to see that it had the revolutionary edge. You don't have to go to Karl Marx to learn how to be a revolutionary. I didn't get my inspiration from Karl Marx; I got it from a man named Jesus, a Galilean saint

who said he was anointed to heal the brokenhearted. He was anointed to deal with the problems of the poor. And that is where we get our inspiration. And we go out in a day when we have a message for the world, and we can change this world and we can change this nation."[6]

Martin Luther King Jr.

King developed a large following while demanding an end to racial restrictions across all of society. And he implored his followers to pair faith in Jesus with nonviolent action to achieve their aims. It was a tactic known as civil disobedience, a peaceful breaking of laws deemed unjust. King explained,

"Nonviolent direct action seeks to create such a crisis and foster such a tension that a community which has constantly refused to negotiate is forced to confront the issue. It seeks to dramatize the issue so that it can no longer be ignored . . . I have earnestly opposed violent tension, but there is a type of constructive, nonviolent tension which is necessary for growth . . . I submit that an individual who breaks a law that conscience tells him is unjust, and who willingly accepts the penalty of imprisonment in order to arouse the conscience of the community over its injustice, is in reality expressing the highest respect for law."[7]

Martin Luther King Jr.

King advocated mass demonstrations, and people followed his lead. They linked arms in a nonviolent movement, which inflicted deep wounds without drawing blood. White-owned businesses lost profits when Black customers boycotted or when Black demonstrators banded together in mass sit-ins. Protests and marches were also employed, drawing attention to injustice while giving White majorities a dreadful sense of lost control.

King's demands for racial equity, along with his willingness to break laws, were far too much too fast for many people. Over and over, King heard the same one-word refrain: *Wait.* Even fellow Christian preachers appealed for slower, less disruptive change. But he believed the time for waiting had long past. With wisdom gained through personal suffering, King frankly explained to those preachers,

"We know through painful experience that freedom is never voluntarily given by the oppressor; it must be demanded by the oppressed. Frankly, I have yet to engage in a direct action campaign that was 'well timed' in the view of those who have not suffered unduly from the disease of segregation. For years now I have heard the word 'Wait!' It rings in the ear of every Negro with piercing familiarity. This 'Wait' has almost always meant 'Never' . . . Perhaps it is easy for those who have never felt the stinging darts of segregation to say, 'Wait.' But when you have seen vicious mobs lynch your mothers and fathers at will and drown your sisters and brothers at whim; when you have seen hate filled policemen curse, kick and even kill your black brothers and sisters; when you see the vast majority of your twenty million Negro brothers smothering in an airtight cage of poverty in the midst of an affluent society; when you suddenly find your tongue twisted and your speech stammering as you seek to explain to your six year old daughter why she can't go to the public amusement park that has just been advertised on television, and see tears welling up in her eyes when she is told that Funtown is closed to colored children, and see ominous clouds of inferiority beginning to form in her little mental sky, and see her beginning to distort her personality by developing an unconscious bitterness toward white people; when you have to concoct an answer for a five year old son who is asking: 'Daddy, why do white people treat colored people so mean?'; when you take a cross county drive and find it necessary to sleep night after night in the uncomfortable corners of your automobile because no motel will accept you; when you are humiliated day in and day out by nagging signs reading 'white' and 'colored'; when your first name becomes 'nigger,' your middle name becomes 'boy' (however old you are) and your last name becomes 'John,' and your wife and mother are never given the respected title 'Mrs.'; when you are harried by day and haunted by night by the fact that you are a Negro, living constantly at tiptoe stance, never quite knowing what to expect next, and are plagued with inner fears and outer resentments; when you are forever fighting a degenerating sense of 'nobodiness'—then you will understand why we find it difficult to wait. There comes a time when the cup of endurance runs over, and men are no longer willing to be plunged into the abyss of despair. I hope, sirs, you can understand our legitimate and unavoidable impatience."[8]

Martin Luther King Jr.

Despite King's pleas, many people still did not see a need for radical change. Wearied by their opposition, King directed some of his harshest criticisms toward supposed White allies who resisted any change they deemed too disruptive. King frankly admitted,

"I must confess that over the past few years I have been gravely disappointed with the white moderate. I have almost reached the regrettable conclusion that the Negro's great stumbling block in his stride toward freedom is not the White Citizen's Counciler or the Ku Klux Klanner, but the white moderate, who is more devoted to 'order' than to justice; who prefers a negative peace which is the absence of tension to a positive peace which is the presence of justice; who constantly says: 'I agree with you in the goal you seek, but I cannot agree with your methods of direct action'; who paternalistically believes he can set the timetable for another man's freedom; who lives by a mythical concept of time and who constantly advises the Negro to wait for a 'more convenient season.' Shallow understanding from people of good will is more frustrating than absolute misunderstanding from people of ill will. Lukewarm acceptance is much more bewildering than outright rejection."[9]

Martin Luther King Jr.

Unsurprisingly, King's verbal assaults ruffled feathers. Concerned about his growing influence and potential ties to communism, the Federal Bureau of Investigation (FBI) extensively wiretapped his phones and bugged his hotel rooms. They succeeded in gathering incriminating evidence, but not of communist ambitions. Instead, they apparently discovered a pattern of marital infidelity and used it to discredit him. The FBI sent a package to King's home with evidence of his offenses, along with a letter insinuating King should commit suicide. It read,

"The American public, the church organizations that have been helping—Protestant, Catholic and Jews will know you for what you are—an evil, abnormal beast. So will others who have backed you. You are done. King, there is only one thing left for you to do. You know what it is . . . There is but one way out for you. You better take it before your filthy, abnormal fraudulent self is bared to the nation."[10]

F.B.I. letter to Martin Luther King Jr.

King was not the only leader who ruffled feathers. Malcolm X, whose indictments against the nation were even harsher than those spoken by King, ruffled even more. Raised in Northern states, Malcolm let no White person off the hook. Nearly everything about him rubbed against the grain of majority opinion and White control.

Born with the name Malcolm Little, his childhood had been rough. Malcolm's father and four uncles were all killed by White men, and his widowed mother struggled to keep the family alive through the Great Depression. On good days, she served meals of oatmeal or cornmeal mush, and on bad days, she could only provide boiled dandelion greens.[11]

By seventh grade, Malcolm was separated from his mom and moved to a predominantly White city, where he was the only Black kid in his class. There, he worked tirelessly to conform, and he succeeded, earning top-notch grades and even being elected class president. But the experience wore him down. He was always treated as a novelty and repeatedly called racial slurs. Under those conditions, the con-

Malcolm X

forming game could only go on for so long. His tipping point came when a teacher asked about his future ambitions. Malcolm proclaimed he wanted to be a lawyer, prompting the teacher to smirk and advise, "Malcolm, one of life's first needs is for us to be realistic. Don't misunderstand me, now. We all here like you, you know that. But you've got to be realistic about being a nigger. A lawyer—that's no realistic goal for a nigger. You need to think about something you *can* be."[12]

Thereafter, Malcolm moved steadily away from schoolwork and toward a life of crime. Eventually, the police caught him in an act of theft, and his next seven years were spent in prison. There, he dedicated himself to a new cause, center-ing his life on religious beliefs. But they did not conform to King's Christianity. Instead, Malcolm converted to a minority sect of Islam, one teaching that White people are a devil race, literally created by an evil scientist.[13] He came to view his birth surname, *Little*, as a mark of evil because it had been handed down from his ancestors' White slave master. So he adopted the last name, *X*, symbolizing the African family name he would never know. That is how Malcolm Little became Malcolm X.

Motivated by his new faith, Malcolm X changed his prior behaviors, renouncing all forms of tobacco, alcohol, narcotics, and premarital sex. And he engrossed himself in books, soaking up everything he could about religion, philosophy, and world history, especially examples of injustice at the hands of White people.

After his release from prison in 1952, he quickly set to work calling Black people to follow Allah, the Islamic word for God, and his messenger, a man by the name of Elijah Muhammed. Those calls were accompanied by relentless attacks against Christianity and White people in general. For instance, he once appealed,

> "Brothers and sisters, the white man has brainwashed us black people to fasten our gaze upon a blond-haired, blue-eyed Jesus! We're worshiping a Jesus that doesn't even *look* like us! Oh, yes! Now just bear with me, listen to the teachings of the Messenger of Allah, The Honorable Elijah Muhammad. Now, just think of this. The blond-haired, blue-eyed white man has taught you and me to worship a *white* Jesus, and to shout and sing and pray to this God that's *his* God, the white man's God. The white man has taught us to shout and sing and pray until we *die*, to wait until *death*, for some dreamy heaven-in-the-hereafter, when we're *dead*, while this white man has his

milk and honey in the streets paved with golden dollars right here on *this* earth!"[14]

Malcolm X

Like King, Malcolm X rebuked people who resisted radical change. But his convictions were born out of a childhood in the North rather than the South. Lashing out against White Northerners, he said,

> "I will pull off that liberal's halo that he spends such efforts cultivating! The North's liberals have been for so long pointing accusing fingers at the South and getting away with it that they have fits when they are exposed as the world's worst hypocrites. I believe my own life *mirrors* this hypocrisy. I know nothing about the South. I am a creation of the Northern white man and of his hypocritical attitude toward the Negro."[15]

Malcolm X

Malcolm X even directly chastised popular Black leaders he believed were too moderate. For instance, when King headlined a March on Washington for Jobs and Freedom,[a] Malcolm X characterized it as the "Farce on Washington" because he believed the march gave a false impression of real change. He refused to celebrate any moderate gains when Black people still had so many wounds and so little power. Reminding people of the work yet to be done, he once fumed,

> "I can't turn around without hearing about some 'civil rights advance'! White people seem to think the black man ought to be shouting 'hallelujah'! Four hundred years the white man has had his foot-long knife in the black man's back—and now the white man starts to

a. King's famous "I Have a Dream" speech was delivered during this March on Washington for Jobs and Freedom in 1963.

wiggle the knife out, maybe six inches! The black man's supposed to be grateful? Why, if the white man jerked the knife out, it's still going to leave a scar!"[16]

Malcolm X

Over a decade of work, Malcolm became known as the "angriest black man in America," and he embraced that label. His messages plainly called Black people to stand together against their common enemy, the White man. And he refused to denounce violence, insisting, "I *am* for violence if non-violence means we continue postponing a solution to the American black man's problem—just to *avoid* violence."[17]

For most of Malcolm's campaign, his message was intentionally racially divisive because he did not support the idea of racial unity. The religious sect to which he adhered taught that racial integration was hopeless. Malcolm wanted to replace forced segregation with voluntary separation, contending the only way to break free from White control was to live apart from White people. That was an irreconcilable difference between Malcolm X's vision and the integrationist hopes of King.

Nevertheless, the two men, both hoping to advance the power held by racial minorities, appealed to overlapping audiences. By the early 1960s, their combined civil rights movements included millions of people spanning all racial groups. Together, they confronted segregation and White control head-on, forcing their way onto headlines worldwide.

Sit-ins, boycotts, and protests abounded. And voting rights took center stage. They worked to register minority voters who had always been discouraged from participating in democracy. Other activists launched a Freedom Rider campaign, forming racially integrated groups who sat together on segregated trains and buses across the South.

Whether riding or marching or sitting, the civil rights movement almost always aligned with King's commitment to non-violence. On rare occasions, demonstrators did act violently, but such instances were dwarfed by the number and brutality of violent White responses. Over and over, peaceful demonstrators were verbally harassed and physically beaten. Their blood was regularly spilled, claiming many lives, yet the movement persisted.

Even King, famous for his commitment to civility, was targeted by violent resistors. Death threats became his new normal, and they were followed by physical attacks. On one occasion, while protesting racial discrimination in housing, King was struck on the head by a rock. After falling to his knees, he gathered himself and continued. On another occasion, in retaliation for King boycotting segregated bus seating, his house was bombed with his wife and infant daughter inside. In response, an angry Black group immediately gathered to defend him, but King implored them to put away their weapons and love their enemies. His words and actions soothed aggressions.

Unfortunately, the same could not be said of law enforcement. They often aroused anger by rubbing salt in open wounds. With woeful regularity, law enforcement forcefully resisted peaceful demonstrators. Fire hoses, billy clubs, dogs, and guns were all used. Many thousands of civil rights activists were arrested. King, himself, was imprisoned many times under trivial charges, including loitering and driving five miles per hour over the speed limit. He was once sentenced to four months in jail after peacefully protesting segregation at a department store. Meanwhile, known White perpetrators of violence walked free, as did public school districts and other government leaders who flippantly dismissed court-ordered desegregation. The law's enforcers had a clear double standard.

∾

The fierce struggle for civil rights continued into 1963, when two Black college students arrived on campus at the University of

Alabama. Nearly a decade had passed since the Supreme Court's school desegregation ruling, yet the state remained defiant in its commitment to segregated education. In fact, just a few months prior, Governor George Wallace had taken office with a rebel cry, declaring, "I draw the line in the dust and toss the gauntlet before the feet of tyranny, and I say segregation now, segregation tomorrow, segregation forever."[18] Federal encroachment upon state rights was the tyranny to which he referred, and he spoke those words from the very spot where Jefferson Davis had been sworn in as President of the Confederacy. The obvious connections between past and present were eerie. Like Jefferson Davis, the governor clung to a lost cause, and history would judge him accordingly. Cameras rolled as he stood at the door of the state's flagship university, personally blocking the students' entrance until federal troops forced him aside.

Making headlines around the world, the spectacle was sure to become a national embarrassment. The sitting president, John F. Kennedy, had to act. No longer could the nation stand still, nor could it continue limiting the pace of progress to a slow crawl. The time had come to either leap forward toward racial equity or step back toward slavery.

Up until this point, President Kennedy had been hesitant to advance civil rights legislation. On this occasion, though, Kennedy boldly answered the call. Before the sun fell on the day of the governor's rebel stand, President Kennedy spoke to the nation in a televised address. Echoing the message of Black leaders, he cast a hopeful vision, appealing for legislators to push beyond token acts to sweeping reform.

> "One hundred years of delay have passed since President Lincoln freed the slaves, yet their heirs, their grandsons, are not fully free. They are not yet freed from the bonds of injustice. They are not yet freed from social and economic

123

oppression. And this Nation, for all its hopes and all its boasts, will not be fully free until all its citizens are free. We preach freedom around the world, and we mean it, and we cherish our freedom here at home, but are we to say to the world, and much more importantly, to each other that this is the land of the free except for the Negroes; that we have no second-class citizens except Negroes; that we have no class or caste system, no ghettoes, no master race except with respect to Negroes? Now the time has come for this Nation to fulfill its promise . . . We face, therefore,

John F. Kennedy

a moral crisis as a country and as a people. It cannot be met by repressive police action. It cannot be left to increased demonstrations in the streets. It cannot be quieted by token moves or talk. It is time to act in the Congress, in your State and local legislative body and, above all, in all of our daily lives . . . Those who do nothing are inviting shame as well as violence. Those who act boldly are recognizing right as well as reality. Next week I shall ask the Congress of the United States to act, to make a commitment it has not fully made in this century to the proposition that race has no place in American life or law."[19]

President John F. Kennedy

President Kennedy's speech was an inspiring reversal of philosophies espoused by his predecessors. Never had a US president advocated for true racial integration, a society where "race has no place." He and other White leaders were learning to sing to a new tune.

And it just so happened that Malcolm X was preparing to sing in harmony. Less than a year after President Kennedy's address, Malcolm would shock the nation by also embracing hope for racial unity. His change of heart came during a pilgrimage to Mecca, the Islamic holy city in Saudi Arabia. There, he worshiped side by side with people of all races and national origins. Recanting the belief that White people are an evil race, he converted to a more common form of Islam and returned to the United States preaching a new message. Malcolm explained,

> "I shared true, brotherly love with many white-complexioned Muslims who never gave a single thought to the race, or to the complexion, of another Muslim. My pilgrimage broadened my scope. It blessed me with a new insight. In two weeks in the Holy Land, I saw what I never had seen in thirty-nine years here in America. I saw all *races*, all *colors*—blue-eyed blonds to black-skinned Africans—in true brotherhood! In unity! Living as one! Worshiping as one! No segregationists—no liberals; they would not have known how to interpret the meaning of those words. In the past, yes, I have made sweeping indictments of *all* white people. I never will be guilty of that again—as I know now that some white people *are* truly sincere, that some truly are capable of being brotherly toward a black man. The true Islam has shown me that a blanket indictment of all white people is as wrong as when whites make blanket indictments against blacks."[20]
>
> *Malcolm X*

Both Malcolm X and President Kennedy, despite their vast differences, eventually cast visions for a racially unified future, and they each significantly influenced the civil rights movement. Sadly, both men were assassinated under mysterious circumstances, adding to the casualties of this era. Conspiracy theories about their respective deaths continue to this day.

President Kennedy's life was cut short before he was able to push civil rights legislation through Congress. He advanced the national dialogue, but ultimately could not overcome a filibuster in the Senate. That challenge would be left to Kennedy's successor, and he was up to the task.

Lyndon B. Johnson took office with an aggressive agenda and an idealistic vision. He told the nation, "For in your time we have the opportunity to move not only toward the rich society and the powerful society, but upward to the Great Society. The Great Society rests on abundance and liberty for all. It demands an end to poverty and racial injustice."[21]

President Johnson was not only idealistic but also politically savvy. And he was resolute in his desire to enact sweeping reform. With Johnson at the helm, a series of transformative legislation passed in the mid-1960s.

The first major step was the Civil Rights Act of 1964. Congressional delegates from former Confederate states voted 115 to 9 *against* it, but delegates from all other states, who voted 353 to 38 for it, overpowered them.[22] Thereafter, federal law would broadly prohibit discrimination and exclusion based on race. No longer could any racial group be explicitly excluded from public accommodations, such as hotels, restaurants, or entertainment venues. Nor could they be excluded from government facilities, such as schools, parks, and libraries. And large employers could no longer legally hire, fire, segregate, or set wages based on race. In short, the Congressional majority decreed people in every city of every state had basic rights to be treated with civility.

Still missing, though, were critical protections of voting rights. To draw attention to this remaining need, activists planned a peaceful march from Selma, Alabama to Montgomery, Alabama early in 1965. Their efforts were successful, but not as they had planned. Soon after the march began, they were attacked by White state troopers and private citizens. Bloody Sunday, as it came to be called, filled newspaper headlines, pressuring Congress to act.[b]

The following week, President Johnson stepped to the podium in a joint session of Congress, adding further pressure,

"Many of the issues of civil rights are very complex and most difficult. But about this there can and should be no argument. Every American citizen must have an equal right to vote. There is no reason which can excuse the denial of that right. There is no duty which weighs more heavily on us than the duty we have to ensure that right. Yet the harsh fact is that in many places in this country men and women are kept from voting simply because they are Negroes . . . What happened in Selma is part of a far larger movement which reaches into every section and state of America. It is the effort of American Negroes to secure for themselves the full blessings of American life. Their cause must be our cause too. Because it is not just Negroes, but really it is all of us, who must overcome

Lyndon B. Johnson

b. A second attempted march, with Martin Luther King Jr. participating, took place two days later. Concerned about violence, King called off the march soon after it began. The march was finally completed later that month under protection from federal troops.

the crippling legacy of bigotry and injustice. And we shall overcome."[23]

President Lyndon B. Johnson

With that last line, "we shall overcome," Johnson unmistakably tied himself to the anthem of the civil rights movement. And then he sung its praise.

> "The real hero of this struggle is the American Negro. His actions and protests, his courage to risk safety and even to risk his life, have awakened the conscience of this nation. His demonstrations have been designed to call attention to injustice, designed to provoke change, designed to stir reform. He has called upon us to make good the promise of America. And who among us can say that we would have made the same progress were it not for his persistent bravery, and his faith in American democracy . . . There have been many pressures upon your President and there will be others as the days come and go. But I pledge you tonight that we intend to fight this battle where it should be fought: in the courts, and in the Congress, and in the hearts of men."
>
> *President Lyndon B. Johnson*

Later that year, Congress passed the Voting Rights Act of 1965. Combined with a recently passed constitutional amendment and a related Supreme Court decision[c], the act significantly removed voter impediments. Poll taxes and knowledge tests were outlawed. Bi-lingual ballots were required. And federal authorities were tasked with registering voters, monitoring voting booths, and invalidating any practices that discriminated by race.

---

c. Refers to the Twenty-fourth Constitutional Amendment and Harper v. Virginia Board of Elections, which both contributed to ending poll taxes.

Lastly, Congress added the Civil Rights Act of 1968, outlawing racial discrimination in housing. No longer could people be legally excluded from residences because of their race. And government agencies, banks, and landlords were instructed to ignore race in underwriting and pricing decisions.

Combined, the civil rights movement and legislative acts of the 1960s achieved far more progress than had been achieved in any decade since Reconstruction. They worked together to remove generations-old legal barriers keeping racial minorities outside the nation's room of White insiders, and they cleared a path leading to truly integrated democracy and capitalism.

The journey to racial equity, though, was unfinished. If Malcolm X was still alive, he would have reminded people they walked around with a knife still six inches into their backs. Even with civil rights, people could still be locked in a state of poverty and powerlessness. And many were. In a repeat of the Reconstruction era, Congress had changed laws to lessen future injustice without addressing the harm caused by past injustice.

Martin Luther King Jr. appealed for greater action. In his mind, phase one of the civil rights struggle was complete and phase two, a much more expensive phase, had not yet begun. In the Spring of 1967, King explained,

> "I think we are in a new era, a new phase of the struggle, where we have moved from a struggle for decency, which characterized our struggle for ten or twelve years, to a struggle for genuine equality. And this is where we are getting the resistance because there was never any intention to go this far . . . And when White Americans tell the Negro to lift himself by his own bootstraps, they don't look over the legacy of slavery and segregation. Now I believe we ought to do all we can and seek to lift ourselves by our own bootstraps. But it's a cruel

gesture to say to a bootless man that he ought to lift himself by his own bootstraps. And many Negroes, by the thousands and millions, have been left bootless as a result of all of these years of oppression and as a result of a society that deliberately made his color a stigma and something worthless and degrading . . . I think the biggest problem now is that we got our gains over the last twelve years at bargain rates, so to speak. It didn't cost the nation anything. In fact, it helped the economic side of the nation to integrate lunch counters and public accommodations. It didn't cost the nation anything to get the right to vote established. And now we are confronting issues that cannot be solved without costing the nation billions of dollars. Now I think this is where we are getting our greatest resistance. They may put it on many other things, but we can't get rid of slums and poverty without it costing the nation something."[24]

Martin Luther King Jr.

Deeper Roots
The War on Poverty

In the 1960s, Congress also launched several major new programs supporting a "war on poverty," declared by President Lyndon B. Johnson. New initiatives included Medicaid to provide health insurance, the Food Stamp Program to address food shortages, Title I funding for schools in low-income communities, and Pell Grants for college students needing financial assistance. But funding for these programs was scant because the government was so focused on resisting communism. Far more tax revenues went to the war in Vietnam, continued build-up of atomic weapons of mass destruction, and space program ambitions to beat the Soviets to the moon. In the 1960s, federal spending on defense and international programs was four times as large as federal payments for individuals (excluding Social Security and Medicare). As a percent of gross domestic product in the 1960s, federal payments for individuals was only 2.5%, which is even less than it was in the 1950s and less than half of its level today.[25]

The increase in such spending over subsequent decades will be revisited in Chapter 11, but there is one simple point I want to note here: as spending increased, taxes did not (see below chart). Congress may have genuinely wanted to help people in poverty, but the data suggests any desire to help was not met by a willingness to sacrifice, either in the form of raising taxes or lowering federal spending elsewhere.

Federal spending increased. Taxes did not.

Total federal receipts and outlays as a %
of gross domestic product (GDP)[26]

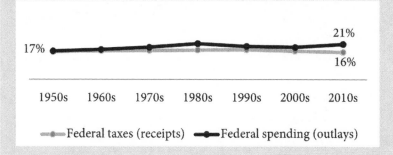

Deeper Roots
Northern Ghettos and Race Riots

The slums to which King referred were primarily in the North, where civil rights legislation had barely addressed the typical daily challenges. Most of the northern Black population lived in impoverished ghettos, with limited employment options, poor transportation and sanitation services, and poorly funded schools. Those challenges were exacerbated by housing shortages, as millions of Black people moved from the South to the North, representing the second phase of their Great Migration. From 1940 to 1970, the portion of the nation's Black population residing in the South plummeted from 77% to 53%.[27] And newcomers to northern cities found few housing options. Their limited wealth, combined with prevalent racial discrimination in housing, restricted them to living in certain parts of the cities.

Empathizing with deep frustrations in ghettos, King advocated for nonviolent protest in the North, like the movement he had led in the South. But not everyone heeded King's advice. In the long, hot summer of 1967, northern discontent turned into violence. There was a chain reaction of riots moving from one city to the next. Cincinnati. Buffalo. Newark. Detroit. Milwaukee. Philadelphia. And so on.

President Lyndon B. Johnson established a commission to research the riots and answer three basic questions: What happened? Why did it happen? And what can be done to prevent it from happening again? The following summer, the commission published findings in a 426-page report, garnering much attention. Over two million copies were quickly sold, and King billed the report as a "physician's warning of approaching death, with a prescription for life."

The report found there had been 164 total civil disorders, some of which turned deadly. Out of about one hundred total deaths, the vast majority were Black civilians. Each incident was different, but there were common themes. Rioters were typically young, poor, and proud of their race. Relative to their non-rioting neighbors, rioters had above-average education. They were highly distrustful of the political and economic systems, but did not reject them. Instead, they were anxious to find their place in them and felt powerless to do so; hence, their call for "black power." And even after the recent string of civil rights legislation, they still saw a dead end in their future.

The report said destructive behavior in the ghetto was the result of continuously building frustrations and disappointments. It plainly rebuked Black perpetrators of violence, while also accusing White people of creating a climate that encourages such behavior. Fingers of blame were pointed at "white terrorism directed against nonviolent protest" and "open defiance of law and federal authority by state and local officials resisting desegregation." As for the cause of ghettos, the commission did not mince words, stating,

> "Segregation and poverty have created in the racial ghetto a destructive environment totally unknown to most white Americans. What white Americans have never fully understood but what the Negro can never forget—is that white society is deeply implicated in the ghetto. White institutions created it, white institutions maintain it, and white society condones it."[28]
>
> *National Advisory Commission on Civil Disorders*

The report went on to call for new actions that were "compassionate, massive and sustained, backed by the resources of the most powerful and the richest nation on this earth." Ultimately, though, the commission's assessment of the situation was sobering. Though Congress had already enacted new civil rights protections, the commission revealed,

"This is our basic conclusion: Our nation is moving towards two societies, one black, one white—separate and unequal . . . We have provided an honest beginning. We have learned much. But we have uncovered no startling truths, no unique insights, no simple solutions."[29]
National Advisory Commission on Civil Disorders

Indeed, the accumulated effects of racial injustice were so great that true reparation would have been enormously expensive. For starters, it would have required a multitude of new school buildings in low-income, minority communities. Ongoing operating expenses for those schools, along with funding for college students, would have been needed as well—not to mention improved housing for minorities, sizable seed money to help them start businesses, and perhaps even a wealth redistribution program.

Had such radical programs been implemented, the lion's share of cost would have been paid by wealthy White families, such as my own. By this point, Warren, my grandfather, had been practicing medicine for more than two decades, and his financial standing had further improved. There was excess, plenty of excess, in the family bank account. Warren was able to give his kids, including my dad, the same privileged childhood he had been afforded. With 1970 approaching, Dad was preparing to begin college. I recently asked him why he went to college, and he responded much like I would.

"Well, it was the presumed thing to do. I don't think it ever occurred to me not to go to college." My dad, like my grandfather, was born on a comfortable path leading to financial security.

The nation was headed in a clear direction. If most White people moved along paths of comfort, while most minorities battled paths with roadblocks, they would not arrive at a common destination. Financial inequalities rooted in injustice would pass to the next generation.

Hoping for a more equitable future, Martin Luther King Jr. continued appealing for phase two of the civil rights struggle. But the harder he pushed, the more he was resisted. The results of Gallup polls tell King's story in a nutshell. Shortly after passage of the Civil Rights Act of 1964, Gallup found 38% of US residents had an unfavorable opinion of King. By 1965, with King insisting voting rights legislation needed to be added, 46% viewed him unfavorably. The following year, as he called for a redirection of national focus away from communism in Vietnam and toward oppressed minorities in the United States, 63% viewed him unfavorably.[30]

Though King's contributions would be celebrated posthumously, popular opinion was against him during his day. In 1968, the man who centered his message on Jesus and an appeal for nonviolence was assassinated. King was murdered at just thirty-nine years of age.

As the 1960s came to end it, the nation stood with one foot in its segregated past and the other in integrationist hopes for the future. People's views on race were messy and evolving. In some cases, genuine affection crossed racial lines, yet affection was not always accompanied by genuine understanding.

My dad's experience was a case in point. His family developed a close bond with Anna Mae Smith, a Black woman. She was their housemaid, serving the Chesney family for about forty years. But she was more than housemaid. Anna Mae became a central figure in Dad's life. They were bonded by mutual affection. When she died in the early 1990s, Dad was asked to speak at her funeral. It was held at an all-Black church, where Dad and a few other Chesneys were the only White people present. He memorialized her with memories from childhood, "For twenty years, she was like my second mom. She hugged me, spanked me, played with me, listened to me, laughed with me, counseled me . . . and made the best fried chicken in all the world."

Anna Mae clearly occupied a special place in Dad's home. And Dad remembers his parents being warm toward Black people in general, certainly never uttering a racial slur. But Dad's perception of Black people was still clouded by the prejudiced customs of the era. For instance, there were segregated bathrooms in his home. The one downstairs, just off the kitchen, was reserved for Anna Mae. The kids could still use it for "standing business," but the only skin to touch that toilet seat was Anna Mae's, presumably because Black and White germs were not supposed to mix.

In addition to such myths, there was indifference, or at least ignorance. During the height of the struggle for civil rights, neither Dad's parents nor his teachers expressed much empathy for the cause. On the other hand, there was much concern about falling property values when a Black family moved into his neighborhood. And civil rights leaders were rarely discussed in Dad's home or at school. Dad cannot recall ever hearing much about Martin Luther King Jr. until he was assassinated. Yet Dad's view of King was still somehow influenced by prevailing racial prejudices. When television news broadcast that King had been assassinated, Dad recalls having the distinct impression that a troublemaker had been killed.

CHAPTER 10

Drifting to Diversity (1970–2020)

BY 1970, THERE was reason for great hope. The nation had reached a turning point, with civil rights legislation aiming to broadly outlaw racial discrimination. Moving forward, minorities were promised new opportunities.

But there were also grave concerns. In the wake of Martin Luther King Jr.'s assassination, racial tension was palpable. Resistance to desegregation continued in many White communities. Hopes remained unfulfilled in many minority communities. And there was still an extreme imbalance of power between the White majority and everyone else. Across the nation, non-Hispanic White people outnumbered all others, five to one. And among members of Congress, they outnumbered minorities by an astounding twenty-seven to one. With such a numeric advantage, the White population controlled every important decision. In short, the United States still operated like a country founded *by* White people *for* White people.

As of 1970, the US population was 83% White, 11% Black, 4% Hispanic, 1% Asian, and 1% American Indian or other. That was the state of the nation when my parents were married in the early 1970s. And it was the nation I was born into just a few years later.

There was little reason to expect the White majority would diminish, yet it did. Over fifty years, from 1970 to today, the nation moved from a state of White dominance toward one of diversity and inclusion. How? There were many factors, but one stands above the rest: Immigration.

~

A famous poem is engraved on a plaque beneath the Statue of Liberty. Speaking words of welcome to immigrants arriving at American shores, it reads,

> Not like the brazen giant of Greek fame,
> With conquering limbs astride from land to land;
> Here at our sea-washed, sunset gates shall stand
> A mighty woman with a torch, whose flame
> Is the imprisoned lightning, and her name
> Mother of Exiles. From her beacon-hand
> Glows world-wide welcome; her mild eyes command
> The air-bridged harbor that twin cities frame.
> "Keep, ancient lands, your storied pomp!" cries she
> With silent lips. "Give me your tired, your poor,
> Your huddled masses yearning to breathe free,
> The wretched refuse of your teeming shore.
> Send these, the homeless, tempest-tost to me,
> I lift my lamp beside the golden door!
>   *The New Colossus, by Emma Lazarus*

When this poem was written in 1883, it gave false hope to many prospective immigrants. Chinese exclusion had just begun, soon to be followed by even tighter immigration restrictions, banning all Asian newcomers. Meanwhile, countries in Northwest Europe were allotted larger immigrant quotas than they could fill.

Throughout the civil rights era, there were calls for immigration reform, and they overlapped with movements for racial equity. The two causes were connected. John F. Kennedy advanced both in his book *A Nation of Immigrants*. Highlighting misalignment between American ideals and existing immigration law, he quipped,

> "The famous words of Emma Lazarus on the pedestal of the Statue of Liberty read: 'Give me your tired, your poor, your huddled masses yearning to breathe free.' Until 1921 this was an accurate picture of our society. Under present law it would be appropriate to add: 'as long as they come from Northern Europe, are not too tired or too poor or slightly ill, never stole a loaf of bread, never joined any questionable organization, and can document their activities for the past two years."[1]
>
> *John F. Kennedy*

Kennedy's book went on to advocate for greater generosity, fairness, and flexibility in immigration policy. He did want to maintain legal control over the flow of immigrants, including numeric limits set by Congress. He also endorsed giving preference to certain types of immigrants over others. But he believed all restrictions associated with nationality and race should be removed. Kennedy proposed replacing national origins quotas with a merit-based system in which "those with the greatest ability to add to the national welfare, no matter where they were born, are granted the highest priority."[2]

In 1965, two years after President Kennedy was assassinated, many of his ideas were written into law. President Lyndon B. Johnson signed the Immigration and Nationality Act of 1965 into law at the foot of the Statue of Liberty, a symbolic location for this historic occasion. The landmark legislation abolished the national origins quota system. Going forward, newcomers could no longer be turned away explicitly because of their race or nationality. Furthermore, immigrants of all races could become citizens.[a]

---

a. The Immigration and Nationality Act of 1952 officially ended Asian exclusion and outlawed racial discrimination in the process of naturalization. But its initial impact was negligible because only a token number of immigrants from Asia were allowed under the quota system. The impact of the 1952 law was greatly magnified by the 1965 law.

Surprisingly, this momentous legislation received relatively little attention. The nation was distracted by the civil rights movement, race riots, and the Vietnam War. Immigration reform was overshadowed. Furthermore, the public was told new immigration guidelines would only have a modest impact. At the signing ceremony, President Johnson insisted, "This bill that we sign today is not a revolutionary bill. It does not affect the lives of millions. It will not reshape the structure of our daily lives."[3] Other leaders shared his assessment. Senator Edward Kennedy promised, ". . . the ethnic mix of this country will not be upset."[4] And Senator Hiram Fong, one of only two Asian senators at the time, anticipated very little immigration from Asia, saying, "the people from that part of the world will never reach one percent of the population . . . our cultural pattern will never be changed as far as America is concerned."[5]

Their projections seemed reasonable, given the context. The number of foreign-born US residents was at an all-time low, representing just 5% of the population in 1970—which remains the lowest mark recorded in any decennial census.[6] A native-born White majority was firmly in control, and few national leaders conceived of a day when White people would not dominate.

As a result, Congress and the president misjudged the impact of immigration reform. Under the new law, more immigrants could come from more places, and they would cause the US population to become a little less White with each passing year. The eventual impacts were inevitable, but not intentional. Congress neither set a target racial mix nor steered demographics in any direction. They only set basic guidelines, then allowed immigration currents to flow as they pleased—at their own pace and in their own direction. Without an oar in the water, the nation began drifting with the current, drifting toward diversity.

What determined the pace and direction of the current? The largest factor, by far, was family reunification. Congress elevated

family members of US residents above all other types of immigrants. The closest relatives of US citizens were admitted regardless of how many applied.[b] More distant relatives were subject to numeric entry limits, but they, too, received preferential treatment.[c] After successfully immigrating to the United States, these immigrants could apply to bring additional family members, allowing extended families to come. Some people call this chain migration.

Congress also prioritized a group called **employment-based immigrants**, most of whom had coveted skills or advanced degrees. Some were executives or managers with multinational companies. And others qualified because they were wealthy investors and were considered to be job creators. These employment-based immigrants were whom President Kennedy had in mind when he proposed a merit-based system. They were his greatest priority because he believed they could immediately add to the national welfare. As he predicted, employment-based immigrants brought valuable knowledge, abilities, and wealth, as well as relationships with influential business partners abroad.

Another notable group of newcomers included **refugees and asylees**.[d] They came to the United States because they faced persecution or a well-founded fear of persecution on account of race, religion, nationality, membership in a particular social group, or political opinion. I believe these were the "huddled masses yearning to breathe free" invited by the poem beneath the Statue of Liberty.

Lastly, there was a varied collection of immigrants who were neither welcomed as family members, nor granted employment-based preferences, nor qualified as refugees or asylees. They had no legal

b. Included spouses, younger children, and parents of US citizens. They still had to pass background checks and complete a tedious application process, but there was no numeric limit applied to this group.
c. Included siblings and older children of US citizens, as well as immediate family members of lawful permanent residents who were not yet US citizens. This class of immigrants sometimes waits in line for many years before they are granted entrance.
d. The basic distinction between refugees and asylees is simple: refugees apply for residence before they come, and asylees apply after they arrive.

path of entry into America, yet they wanted to come to find greater opportunity, freedom, and safety. Their best hope was to emulate the early European immigrants by arriving unannounced. So that is what they did. And they came by the millions. Without being granted permission, they came. Outside the bounds of immigration law, they came. Lacking government-approved documentation, they came. If they could not gain entry by day, they came by night. The largest number crossed the southern border into Southwestern states, those that used to be part of Mexico. Then they established new lives in the shadows as unauthorized immigrants.

Over time, their presence became too large to hide and too helpful to begrudge. Many US businesses, especially in the agricultural industry, were propelled by the relatively inexpensive labor unauthorized immigrants provided. And businesses could recruit them openly because there were no federal laws against hiring unauthorized immigrants.

By the mid-1980s, the count of unauthorized immigrants rose to several million. Understandably, such widespread defiance of immigration law became a hot topic in Congress. There were calls for stricter border enforcement and penalties for employers of unauthorized immigrants. But the agricultural industry worried such action would deplete their labor force, and immigrant advocates were fearful of discrimination against Hispanic workers.

After several solutions to the dilemma were rebuffed in Congress, a compromise was finally reached in 1986. Named the Immigration and Control Act, it was framed as a three-legged stool. First, there would be tougher border enforcement, including greater funding for border patrol and criminal penalties for people aiding unauthorized immigrants. Second, businesses would be required to verify their employees were lawful residents, and non-compliant businesses could be fined. Third, unauthorized immigrants already living in the United States would be brought out of the shadows—made permanent legal residents.[e]

In this compromise, lawmakers hoped they had found a long-term solution to the problem of illegal immigration. Moments before signing the bill into law, President Ronald Reagan said its objective was to "establish a reasonable, fair, orderly, and secure system of immigration," and predicted, "Future generations of Americans will be thankful for our efforts to humanely regain control of

Ronald Reagan

our borders."[7] These goals, however, would not be met. Before long, unauthorized immigrants would once again number in the millions because border control remained elusive after the Immigration and Control Act. People continued to come illegally after 1986 for the same reasons they had come before; the potential reward of a better life was worth the risk of being caught and deported. Likewise, US employers continued hiring unauthorized immigrants because the financial rewards from employing them were worth the risk of being caught and fined.[f]

---

e. The act included two separate programs providing permanent resident status, commonly called amnesty or legalization. One was available to unauthorized immigrants who had already lived in the United States for at least five years when the bill was passed. The other was a special provision to help the agriculture industry retain its workforce, and it was available for agricultural workers who had lived in the United States for as little as 90 days.

f. In the early 1990s, an additional legal path for entry was opened for people who did not fit into family-based, employment-based, or refugee and asylee classes. But it did not stop the inflow of unauthorized immigrants because the newly opened path was extremely narrow. Called the *Diversity Visa Program*, or the *green card lottery*, it admitted less than 1% of its applicants each year. Furthermore, only certain people were even allowed to apply because the program was restricted to countries with low rates of immigration. Residents of countries with high rates of immigration, such as Mexico and India, were ineligible for the Diversity Visa Program.

Throughout the 1990s and into the 2000s, national borders remained porous, and employment opportunities in the United States continued drawing unauthorized immigrants. After arriving, they worked hard, employers profited from their labor, and consumers benefited from their services. They made new friends, adjusted to new culture, and learned the English language. Their children were born and raised here as US citizens. This country became their home, and they blended with those who had legally immigrated.

~

The total number of people who immigrated over these fifty years was tremendous. From 1970 to 2020, more than forty million people established *legal* permanent residence. Additionally, more than ten million are here now illegally, as unauthorized immigrants.[8] Combining those who came legally with those here illegally, more than fifty million people arrived over fifty years.

In addition to being tremendous in size, they were also tremendous in diversity. Immigrants came from all over the world, bringing new cultures and experiences with them.

About half arrived from countries to the south of the United States, including Mexico, the Caribbean, South America, and Central America. By ethnicity, most of this group identifies as Hispanic or Latino. By race, most call themselves White or prefer not to identify with any racial group, though some call themselves Black, American Indian, or Asian. Most arrived with below average wealth and education, by US standards, though some came with wealth and advanced degrees. Their languages varied, too. Spanish and English were the most common, and some were raised speaking Portuguese or French-based creole. They are a diverse group.

The second largest group of newcomers arrived from Asia, the greatest number from the Philippines, India, China, Vietnam, and Korea, in that order. They, too, had a myriad of backgrounds, yet they were sometimes mischaracterized as a uniform group. Asian people in the United States came to be regarded as a "model minority" because their average education and income exceeded that of other minority groups. And this notion of a model minority fed racial biases by suggesting other minority groups were somehow inferior. People advancing beliefs in a racial hierarchy, with Asians at the top, overlooked a simple fact: Asian immigrants were not a random sample of Asian people in this world. Rather, they were the chosen ones, so to speak. A large share of them, far more than any other immigrant group, were admitted as employment-based immigrants, already having advanced degrees, coveted skills, or significant wealth. There was a direct connection between their path of entry and their ultimate success.[8,9]

After the group from Asia, the next largest group came from Europe, representing about 13% of all immigrants. And the final sizable group arrived from Africa. This last group represented only about 5% of all newcomers, but their historic relevance was greater than their count. They were the first large wave of voluntary immigrants from Africa to America. Unlike the Africans brought as captives in the hulls of slave ships, this new wave of African newcomers chose America of their own free will.[h,10]

---

g. From 2006–2017, 55% of all people granted lawful permanent residence as employment-based immigrants came from Asia.

h. Percentages reflect the distribution of new legal permanent residents by location of their last residence, from 1965–2017.

Most immigrants came as reuniting family members.

New lawful permanent residents by admission class, 2000–2017[11]

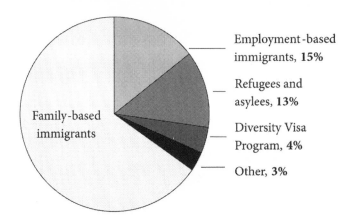

Family-based immigrants

Employment-based immigrants, **15%**

Refugees and asylees, **13%**

Diversity Visa Program, **4%**

Other, **3%**

And they were tremendous in both number and diversity.

New lawful permanent residents by last residence, 1970–2017[12]

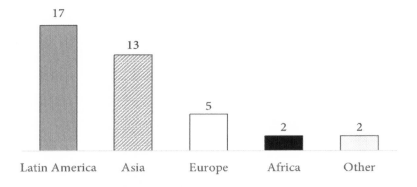

17 — Latin America
13 — Asia
5 — Europe
2 — Africa
2 — Other

With their arrival, the United States drifted toward diversity.

US population distribution by race and ethnicity[13]

		1970	2019	Change
☐	White (non-Hispanic)	83%	60%	-23%
■	Black	11%	13%	2%
▨	Hispanic	4%	18%	14%
▧	Asian	1%	6%	5%
▢	Other	1%	3%	2%

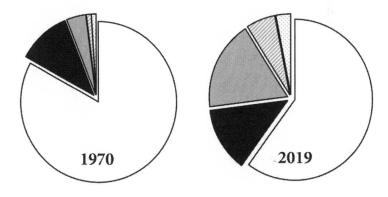

As a tremendously large and diverse group, these fifty million immigrants, plus their millions of US-born children, transformed national demographics, but not all at once. The shift was slow and steady. I think about it like my own process of aging. Each morning when I look in the mirror, I see the same person I saw the day before. Physical changes occurring over a single day are too small to notice. Aging is only obvious over a much longer time frame. For me, five years is more than enough. Just that long ago, my hair was solid brown, and now I have too many grey hairs to count. Aging happened bit by bit and changed the face of who I am.

Similarly, the movement toward diversity was not always noticed because it happened in small steps. And many steps in the same direction covered an enormous distance. The half-century from 1970 to 2020 brought the greatest demographic change this nation has ever seen. No other period even comes close. The foreign-born portion of the population surged. From its historical low of 5%, it returned nearly to a historical high of 15%. The non-Hispanic White share of the population plummeted from 83% to 60%, and the minority share swelled from 17% to 40%, driven by growing Hispanic and Asian numbers.

How significant were those movements? Their impact is difficult to overstate. Civil rights gains may have stalled or reversed without the drift toward diversity. Instead, something new began happening after 1970. Across boundaries of race and ethnicity, people began coming together.

CHAPTER 11

Coming Together
(1970–2020)

IT IS SAID the United States is like a melting pot. Here, people from around the world come together. Old allegiances fade, and new joint identities are formed. The descendants of bitter enemies can even become neighbors. At least, that is the idealistic notion.

The melting pot may accurately depict how people in America came together within racial groups, but not across them. For several centuries, segregating barriers prevented other colors from melting into White. Not until the civil rights era were those barriers significantly deconstructed and, by then, society was deeply fragmented along racial lines, with 98% of all wealth still held by White people.[1] So even with new civil rights legislation in place, melting together across racial lines would not happen quickly. It *could not* happen quickly. Coming together would require significant actions to lift up minorities who had been pushed down for so long.

Fortunately, many such actions were taken. And some of them were expensive. Numerous federal benefits were launched in the 1960s and repeatedly expanded over future decades. Today, the largest category of aid is health care, accounting for more than half of all federal assistance for people with low income. Next is direct cash aid, either as recurring payments to people with physical disabilities or as tax credits for low-income workers. There is also food aid, as well as federal assistance for education, housing, and social services. In total, the federal government now spends nearly one trillion dollars annually on benefits and services for people with low income.

The federal government spends nearly one trillion dollars each year on benefits and services for people with low income.[2]

Category	2018 Federal Spending ($ billions)	% of Total
Health Care	$ 518	56%
Cash Aid	146	16%
Food Aid	94	10%
Housing and Development	54	6%
Education	52	6%
Social Services	43	5%
Other	11	1%
Total	$ 918	100%

And such spending has risen considerably over recent decades.

Annual federal payments to individuals (excluding Medicare and Social Security) as a percent of gross domestic product.[3]

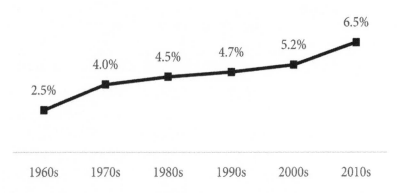

2.5%	4.0%	4.5%	4.7%	5.2%	6.5%
1960s	1970s	1980s	1990s	2000s	2010s

Actions were also taken to improve job opportunities for minorities. Federal agencies, which were spending billions of dollars on contracts with private companies that employed nearly all-White workforces, introduced new guidelines requiring contracted companies to take affirmative action to diversify their workforces. For instance, companies could set racial diversity goals and timetables for achieving them.

Educational institutions enacted similar measures. In admissions offices, many colleges considered the race of applicants in efforts to achieve greater diversity among student populations. They still do. At some colleges, average entrance test scores are permitted to be lower for Black and Hispanic students or required to be higher for White and Asian students. The fairness of such practices is still hotly debated today, and the legality is sure to be argued in courts for years to come.

Large businesses also acted. Recognizing their workforces were Whiter than their customer bases, many companies added diversity and inclusion to their key objectives. They monitored hiring practices to guard against racial discrimination and devised new recruiting strategies to increase hiring of minorities. In their offices, some companies launched affinity groups or minority leadership programs to help retain and advance the careers of minority workers.

These collective actions taken in government, education, and the private industry were significant. Perhaps even more impactful, though, was the dynamic duo of civil rights and the nation's drift toward diversity. Those two forces worked together to propel positive change. With greater legal rights and larger population numbers, minorities grew more visible to the majority White population. Inevitably, they became more familiar, less foreign. As social interactions crossed racial bounds with greater frequency, long-standing social norms became antiquated.

My home city, Greensboro, North Carolina, serves as a prime example. As of 1970, the city was about 70% White and 30% Black, with very little racial integration. Most people stayed on their own side of racial dividing lines, and wounds from contentious civil rights struggles were fresh. Just a few years prior, when Whites-only signs still hung in store windows, four Black college students had been refused service at a downtown lunch counter. When the Greensboro Four, as they came to be called, risked their lives to demand civil treatment, they started a sit-in protest that spread nationwide. And the movement succeeded. Local businesses were forced to open their doors to all races. These gains were subsequently solidified and extended as the city diversified. Over the next fifty years, the Black population significantly increased, and sizable Hispanic and Asian populations arrived. Today, Greensboro is about 40% White[a] and 40% Black, with most of the remainder being Hispanic or Asian.[4] With such tremendous diversity, integrated dining lost its taboo. The lunch counter where sit-in protests began is now a museum. Surrounding it on all sides are new restaurants, part of an ongoing revitalization of our downtown. I stroll by this area regularly, just a couple blocks from my office. Gone are the Whites-only signs and attitudes. Racial dividing lines have faded, fears and biases subsided. I can now dine downtown with friends of any race without so much as turning a head. Greensboro remains far from perfect, but it has undoubtedly come a long way.

Increased racial diversity and integration took hold in other cities as well. Minorities, once segregated as threats, became important customers and partners to White business owners. As minority buying power increased, White business owners spent less time resenting minority success and more time trying to profit from it. Consumer products now increasingly cater to diverse audiences.

Minorities even took center stage where they had once been excluded as outsiders. In the entertainment industry, many surged

---

a. Excludes White residents who also identify as Hispanic.

to the top and set new standards. Minority actors and musicians became icons with broad-based appeal. College and professional sports teams likewise transitioned from banning minority players to aggressively recruiting them.

Importantly, diversity also expanded in government. In Congress, minority representation increased from 4% in 1970 to 22% in 2020.[5] And there has even been a change in posture among White elected officials. Appealing for support from a diverse electorate, many White candidates shifted their platforms to address, or at least validate, concerns commonly voiced by minority voters.

The general well-being of minorities greatly improved, as well. Childhood school enrollment and adult literacy approached 100%, and opportunities for college education expanded. With better education and more inclusive workplaces, incomes grew. From 1970 to today, average income for minorities rose more than 50%, even after adjusting for inflation.[6] Life expectancy soared, too. In 1900, minorities could expect to live only thirty-three years, and now they can expect to live about eighty years.[b,7] In short, both the quality and quantity of life have markedly improved for people of all races.

∼

During my early research for this book, I encountered one unique case of coming together across racial lines. My sister, whom I had recently told about our family's connection to slavery, left me a vague voicemail, providing only enough information to generate intrigue. I took the bait and quickly returned her call. Getting right to the point, she explained one of her coworkers shares our last name, Chesney, and is directly related to us. But not by blood. Our bond is rooted in our shared history. Her coworker is a descendant of Pharaoh Chesney, the man my ancestors enslaved. Adding another layer to this story, my sister and I are not blood relatives

---

b. Life expectancy at birth, in years, as of 2017: Hispanic 82, White 79, Black 75. Data for Asian people was not provided.

either. For thirty years, ever since she joined our family as an infant, she has been my sister, but we look nothing alike. She was born in Korea and adopted into my family. So my sister, her coworker, and I had an odd connection. We share no blood relation, and we identify with three different racial groups—Asian, Black, and White—yet we trace our last name to the same man—John Chesney, enslaver of Pharaoh.

Prior to my sister's finding, I did not have any direct connections to Pharaoh's descendants. Before publishing a book about our shared history, I needed to build those bridges. I wanted at least a couple people from Pharaoh's family to validate my version of events and have an opportunity to express any concerns. I also wanted to begin a relationship with them, not as a means to an end, but as an end in itself.

I searched through family trees on an ancestry website and identified a few living descendants. That step was easy, but the next one—picking up the phone—felt less comfortable. Our shared history is not a pleasant one, and I worried about how to start the conversation.

Generations removed from the injustice of slavery, connections to the past are still disturbing. Unhealthy impulses told me to hide from the past and ignore its impact on the present. Openly acknowledging the sins of my ancestors could put a stain on my family name. It could hurt my brand, so to speak. It could even reveal links between injustice and my own financial success.

But the healthier side of me wanted to listen and learn, without focusing on self-interest. There is freedom in embracing truth and lowering emotional walls of defense. So I called.

The approach I chose was direct and honest. I explained that we share a last name because my great-great-great-grandfather once enslaved their ancestors, and I told them about the book I was writing, the one you now hold in your hands.

Had they hung up the phone, uninterested in engaging with me, a stranger connected to tragic injustice in their family tree, I would not have blamed them. But that's not what happened. Proving my pre-call worries needless, they stayed on the line. The people with whom I spoke were warm and inviting. They were interested in my studies, glad to have me write about our families, and willing to help. We connected first by phone and email, and then in-person over shared meals. I even talked with the wife of Paul Chesney, great-grandson of Pharaoh. Sadly, Paul died thirty years ago. His wife, now in her nineties, was a delight. Her daughter, too, was kind and helpful.

They knew more about my family than I had known about theirs. Paul's daughter knew my grandfather and aunt by name. As it turns out, Paul did yardwork in my dad's childhood neighborhood, and even at Dad's house, in the mid-1900s. That visual image shook me. A century removed from the days of slavery, the descendant of a Chesney slave was doing yardwork for the descendant of a Chesney enslaver. The story of race is a continuous strand running through my family tree.

As I learned about Black Chesney families, I also recognized vast differences between today and past eras. In the first half of the 1900s, the Black side of Chesney family trees was strictly segregated under the law. Today, they benefit from greater legal protections and economic opportunities. Pharaoh's living descendants are now teachers, artists, veterinarians, doctors, janitors, waitresses, engineers, business owners, musicians, and much more.

After our first meal together, I picked up the bill. After our second, *they* paid for *me*.

~

Clearly, this nation is far different than it was when my grandparents were born in the early 1900s. Or when my parents were born in the 1950s. Or when I was born in 1980. In my opinion, it is a much better nation, one that has traveled a long distance down a path toward racial equity. Along the way, there have been too many milestones reached to list here, but one more bears mention.

This remarkable event occurred in 2008, barely a century after President Theodore Roosevelt was assailed for merely dining with Booker T. Washington. In Roosevelt's day, public dismay sent a clear message: The White House was for White people. By the time voters arrived at polls in 2008, public sentiment and national demographics had shifted toward diversity and inclusion. More White voters were receptive to minority leadership, and there were more minority voters to be heard.

Barack Obama

Presidential candidate Barack Obama, a Black man, received broad support. From the Black community, he won an astounding 95% of votes cast. Support was also strong from other minority groups. He was selected by 67% of Hispanic voters and 62% of Asian voters. He was not the top choice of the White electorate, receiving only 43% support, but even that amount marked a significant break from the past.[8] When any of my ancestors were born, Obama could not have even made it on the ballot.

Yet when my children were born, he was sitting in the Oval Office. Fifty-three percent of all voters in the United States of America voted for a Black man to be their foremost leader. Soak that in for a minute. Think about where this nation began and how far it has come. By majority will of the voting public, the White House became home to a Black family.

CHAPTER 12

Staying Apart
(2020)

ON A LONG journey away from slavery, the United States has arrived at its ultimate destination, one of equity. Long ago, awful racial injustices did happen, but the past is in the past. The election of a Black president proved that to be the case. New game rules are in place, and they are beyond fair for racial minorities. Everyone now benefits from broad legal protections against discrimination, and everyone is included as insiders in capitalism and democracy. If anything, the tables have turned, such that minorities now have the easiest path to success. And those who cannot get by on their own receive ample assistance from the government. So complaints about racial injustice and unequal opportunities are no longer warranted.

I often encounter suggestions like those. They did not used to bother me, but now they do because I recognize they are based on half-truths. Walking through the story of race, I came to see the other half, and it helped me understand long-standing racial tensions.

In the late 1960s, leaders bitterly disagreed about the state of our nation. Martin Luther King Jr. insisted the journey toward racial equity had only just begun, while others believed it was complete. Five decades later, the same basic debate remains. As a nation, have we reached a place of equity, or is there still some distance left to travel?

Thus far in this book, I have tried to withhold personal opinions. Admittedly, I sometimes failed in that endeavor because my perspective inevitably slanted my choice of content. After all, there is no unbiased or complete version of history; there are only incomplete narratives told by biased people. Nevertheless, I did try to keep my opinions to myself. In the remaining pages, I will take a different approach. As I reflect on the present day and look to the future, I will openly incorporate my own views. You will likely agree with some and disagree with others, and that is fine. I have yet to meet a person with whom I always agree.

To start, let me tell you what I see when I look across America. I see a nation that stayed apart even as it came together. We are still divided, deeply divided, by race, and I believe our ultimate destination has not been reached.

Recently, I participated in a group exercise with twenty-five local leaders in business, government, and non-profit. I was one of just a few White men in the diverse group, and we were engaged in an all-day discussion about race. Late in the day, the group facilitator asked us to each write a few words we had "read, seen, or heard" about certain people groups, which she would name. Those were the extent of her instructions. Then she began reading her list, pausing only briefly between each group, "Black, Asian, Hispanic, Native American, Middle Eastern, White." There was not much time to think, so I scribbled the first couple words that came to mind for each people group. Other participants did the same. Then our anonymous scribble was collected.

The following fifteen minutes I will long remember. We listened in somber silence as every response was read aloud. The facilitator had not asked for negative descriptors, but that was what we mostly provided. Black people were lazy, dangerous, drug addicts, poor, resourceful, resilient, and uneducated. Asian people were foreigners, timid, tech savvy, smart, and poor communicators. Native Americans were drunks, savages, gamblers, warriors, and superstitious. Hispanic people were illegals, manual laborers, good cooks, drug dealers, hard workers, and housekeepers. Middle Easterners were terrorists, belly dancers, oppressors of women, and extremists. And White people were greedy, unaware, privileged, racist, controlling, and proud.

Those are just a few responses I remember. The actual lists were much longer, and they were shocking. Yet they were also familiar, which created palpable discomfort in the room. As a group, we recognized our heads are filled with biases, and even if we do not consciously believe them, they impact us. They flash to the front of our minds as we meet new people and encounter new scenarios. We may judge people based on stereotypes before learning about them as individuals. Or, based on race, we may choose whether to embrace new acquaintances as prospective friends or cautiously approach them as strangers. And biases can easily influence any decision relying on so-called gut feel—like choosing whether to trust a salesperson, considering intangible factors in hiring decisions, or selecting a contractor for a home renovation job. The possibility of racial bias impacting mindsets and actions may seem benign, but it is a destructive cancer. It furthers division by preventing us from participating in society as equals.

One especially damaging demonstration of bias is the characterization of people as insiders and outsiders. I particularly see this type of injustice hurting Hispanic and Asian people. Their doors of entry into the United States widened with immigration reform, but the doors only led across the nation's border, not into its inner circle. Too often, Hispanic and Asian residents are treated as foreigners who do not belong here, and their rising numbers are begrudged.

Pushed furthest to the outside are those who came illegally, whose situations are complex. On one hand, they broke the law to gain admittance. There is no way around that giant elephant in the room. Personally, I do believe lack of border control is concerning because law and order are essential to national peace and prosperity. At the same time, I recognize unauthorized immigrants came and stayed because they were wanted. They were wanted by employers who depend on their labor and cannot find suitable alternatives, wanted by consumers who purchase goods and services subsidized by their low wages, and wanted by people who became their close friends or romantic partners. Unauthorized immigrants are here because they are wanted by at least some insiders, even as others simultaneously seek them for deportation. That conflict is part of their daily lives.

Many who were born here as citizens or immigrated legally face similar challenges. On paper, they are American insiders, as much so as I am, yet many of them are accustomed to being treated as aliens. Often, they are falsely assumed to be unauthorized immigrants, which makes little sense. Seven out of every eight Hispanic and Asian residents of the United States are here legally, so it is only logical to assume an individual is here legally until proven otherwise.

Regardless of how they come or how long they live here, many Hispanic and Asian Americans struggle to be heard in inner circles of leadership. It seems to me they are overlooked because they are deemed "less American" on account of their race or ethnicity. And those viewed as "most American" are people like me, people who are accepted as White.

From this country's founding to today, minorities have always been underrepresented in positions of power. In Congress, their representation has not increased as quickly as their overall share of the population. Today, the 22% minority share of Congress is far below the 40% minority share of the US residents. In the rooms where laws are written, White people are significantly overrepresented, Black people slightly underrepresented, and Hispanic and Asian people substantially underrepresented.[1]

Minorities are still underrepresented in Congress[2]

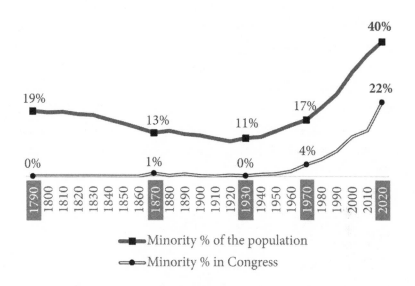

Minority % of the population
Minority % in Congress

... especially Hispanic and Asian people.

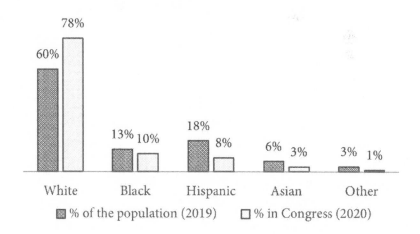

% of the population (2019)   % in Congress (2020)

Another showing of persistent racial division is the lack of diversity in residential areas, which lessens opportunities for inter-racial friendships. Segregation keeps racial groups divided, not only physically, but also ideologically.

In the three Southern states where I have lived, communities that are diverse in total are still segregated by neighborhood. The initial cause of that segregation was explained by the federal government in 1973, shortly after racial discrimination in housing had been outlawed. The bipartisan US Commission on Civil Rights confessed,

> "The patterns of racial residence we have today are a legacy of the past, in which discrimination, not choice or ability to pay, has been the principal factor that determines where minority families live. It is a national history in which Government and private industry came together to create a system of residential segregation. Residential segregation is so deeply ingrained in American life that the job of assuring equal housing opportunity to minority groups means not only eliminating present discriminatory practices but correcting the mistakes of the past as well."[3]
>
> *US Commission on Civil Rights*

Sadly, the consequences persist today, fifty years later. Recall the map I showed in the first chapter, the one illustrating a stark divide between the northwest and southeast portions of my home city. The former is mostly White and wealthy, and the latter is largely Black and financially poor. When I recreated the same map for 1970 and held it beside the one representing today, the connection between the two was obvious. Neighborhoods were forcefully segregated before 1970, and even as the city's total population diversified, racial dividing lines remained.

And even diverse cities are still segregated by neighborhood.

White population % by census tract in Greensboro, NC[4]

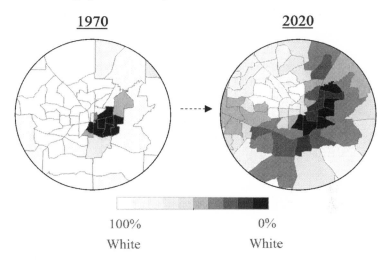

1970 → **2020**

100%   0%
White   White

Much of the reason segregation continues today relates to household finances. Between racial groups, there are huge and long-standing racial disparities in financial well-being.

Today, White families across the nation earn about 60% more income, on average, than do Black families, and that gap is a bit worse than it was in 1970. As for differences in wealth, White families have about seven times as much as Black families, just as they did in 1970. The gap in home ownership rates also remained wide. Seventy-six percent of White families own their homes, verses only 47% of Black families.

In short, there is still an enormous imbalance in the nation's prosperity. Compared to the White population, the Black population still has far less to spend on nutrition, safety, and entertainment, and they still have far less to invest in homes and business ventures.

Racial gaps in financial well-being are large. They have not closed, and it seems they are not closing. They were created unjustly prior to 1970; I do not believe that is debatable. And they have remained in place since; also not debatable. So I view them as a direct legacy of past injustice, much like residential segregation. The two go hand in hand.

Racial disparities in financial well-being have not improved

*Average **family income** by race of householder, adjusted for inflation*[5]

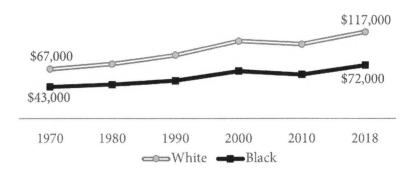

*Average White family **wealth** relative to Black family wealth*[6]

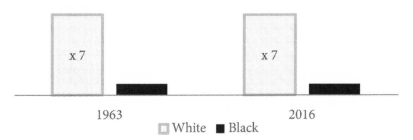

*Rates of **homeownership** by race of householder[a,7]*

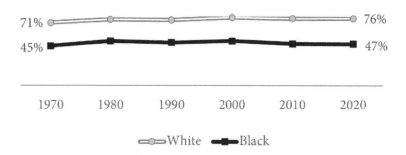

| 71% | | | | | | 76% |
| 45% | | | | | | 47% |

1970 1980 1990 2000 2010 2020

 White Black

These legacies are apparent among the several hundred living descendants of John Chesney and Pharaoh Chesney. I do not know most of them, but I have studied family trees enough to recognize their names in the local phone book—surprisingly, printed phone books do still exist! Judging by home addresses, prosperity remains far more common among John's descendants than it does among Pharaoh's.

Knowing what I do of John and Pharaoh, I would rather have Pharaoh's genes. He seems to have been the physically stronger and mentally sharper one. But he was enslaved on account of his race, his descendants were legally oppressed for another century, and still, today, they live in a land where racial biases cut deep. As we broke bread together, they trusted me with their stories. I listened to them recall times when they were excluded from venues or otherwise mistreated because of their race, and I learned of painful feelings aroused by today's news headlines. Some wounds are still open. As William Faulkner once wrote, "The past is never dead. It's not even past."

∽

There seems to be much confusion about why racial gaps have not closed. I often encounter arguments that go something like

a. Not shown in the graph: For 2Q 2020, the homeownership rate was 51% for Hispanic people and approximately 61% for Asian people.

this: "Nobody alive today was born into pre-Civil War slavery, and everyone now benefits from strong legal protections against discrimination. If natural born potential is similar across racial groups, shouldn't financial outcomes also be similar?"

I will address those questions with a simple illustration. Suppose there is a race between two runners, one starting from ahead and running with the wind and the other starting from behind and running against the wind. If these runners have similar work ethic and abilities, should they be expected to finish in a tie? Of course not, as they face extremely different circumstances.

Likewise, the Black and Hispanic populations started from behind and have remained behind. With less money, less education, and less control of government, they have long been running against the wind. Through luck, genius, or superior efforts, some people do overcome disadvantaged circumstances to achieve prosperity. Far more often, though, poverty passes from one generation to the next, regardless of race.

To understand how this might happen, consider a family with two children and two working parents, both of whom work forty hours per week, fifty-two weeks per year, without ever taking a week off. If they each earn ten dollars per hour, well above the federal minimum wage, then this family's annual income would be forty-two thousand dollars. You might assume they would receive extensive federal assistance, but likely they would not. They earn too much to qualify for benefits like health insurance (Medicaid) and food assistance (SNAP). This hypothetical family is not uncommon. It is typical. Nationally, about 40% of Black and Hispanic families make less than this amount, and they face hardships unknown to people higher up the income ladder. Meals with balanced nutrition may be out of their reach, and home Internet access may not fit in the budget. They may not be able to afford a personal automobile or even basic home maintenance. Sicknesses may last longer because doctor's visits and costly medication are avoided. The kids may need to be left alone while the parents work, and life may take a heavy emotional toll. Stress from poor nutrition, financial worries, and physical threats can compound on one another, making self-confidence and optimism difficult to maintain.

Kids from low-income families face obstacles at school as well. Many attend schools in low-income communities, which have the greatest educational needs, yet often operate with the tightest budgets. Under the public school funding model, only about 10% of total funding comes from the federal government. The rest is provided by states and cities, and low-income school districts naturally collect less tax revenues, so they have less money to spend on education. Sadly, the very kids who need the most support often get the least funding.

A different dilemma occurs within school districts, where funding is often distributed relatively evenly across schools on a per student basis. Some people believe this funding model is fair. Others argue far greater funding should go to kids with greater needs. I lean toward the latter.

Given the wide range of childhood experiences, both at home and at school, differences in educational outcomes by race should come as no surprise. White and Asian kids, with higher average family income, score the best on standardized tests. And Black and Hispanic students score much lower. Those differences carry over to college, with a far greater portion of White and Asian kids obtaining degrees.

The bottom line is White and Asian kids tend to receive greater privileges, while Black and Hispanic kids tend to face greater obstacles.

Educational outcomes vary greatly by race.

Average __SAT scores__ for graduating high school seniors in 2018[8]

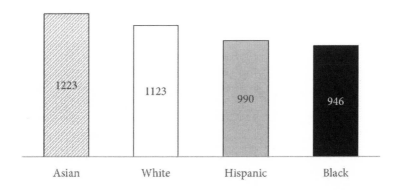

Percent of adults (age 25+) who have completed __college__[b,9]

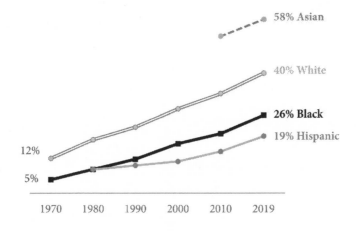

b. Some Asian and Hispanic data points are missing due to lack of data.

And there is an even more uncomfortable truth, one that further explains why many minorities still lag behind. Historically, racial injustice has been a crime without a penalty. People guilty of the most grievous acts are now dead, but the consequences of their actions live on because they were not rectified. Our nation's history is one of gradually making laws fairer without addressing the consequences of past unfairness.

One notable exception came in 1988, when the federal government took responsibility for a major wrongdoing. Congress admitted guilt for unjustifiably incarcerating Japanese Americans during World War II, and then reinforced words with dollars. More than forty years after the injustice occurred, Congress attempted to reckon with the past by giving twenty thousand dollars to each victim's family.

I sometimes wonder what would have transpired over the last one hundred and fifty years had the Black population been given significant land, financial assets, and top-notch educational opportunities after the Civil War; or how the last fifty years might have played out if provisions of life-transformative scale had been given to minorities during the civil rights era. Such interventions never happened.

Of course, many federal programs of assistance were indeed launched in the 1960s. Several of those were highlighted in the previous chapter, but they came with a couple important caveats. First, they only provided basic provisions, such as healthcare and subsidized housing, not life-transformative investments, such as free land or large seed capital for new business ventures. Second, they were not directed at minorities.[c,10] After a couple centuries of discriminating *against* racial minorities, the federal government was unwilling to discriminate *for* them when it came to entitlement benefits. Assistance went to all people in need, regardless of race,

---

c. In 1970, Black people represented only 11% of the total US population. Thus, though Black people were three times as likely as White people to be in poverty, the total distribution of those in poverty was 69% White and 30% Black. So most funding for new federal benefits went to White people.

and, in that sense, it was fair. But little consideration was given to the causes of poverty. More specifically, the federal government did not give greater levels of assistance to individuals hurt by racial injustice, and one could argue that was unfair.

Furthermore, some government interventions exacerbated existing racial disparities. Such was the case with a so-called *war on drugs* launched around 1970. At the time, marijuana and LSD were popular in hippie culture, and heroin use was common in urban areas and among US soldiers in Vietnam. Then came growth in cocaine use; the more expensive powder form flourished in high income communities while the less expensive rock form, called crack, grew more popular in low income communities. Drugs reached across barriers of race and income.

In the White House, concerns mounted. President Nixon declared illegal drugs to be "America's public enemy number one," and subsequent administrations added to Nixon's self-proclaimed "all-out offensive."[11]

A major escalation in the war on drugs came in 1986, when President Ronald Reagan and First Lady Nancy Reagan delivered a stirring address from a couch in the White House. Broadcast in living rooms nationwide, she pleaded,

> "Today, there is a drug and alcohol abuse epidemic in this country, and no one is safe from it. Not you, not me, and certainly not our children, because this epidemic has their names written on it . . . Drugs take away the dream from every child's heart and replace it with a nightmare, and it's time we in America stand up and replace those dreams . . . There's no moral middle ground. Indifference is not an option. We want you to help us create an outspoken intolerance for drug use. For the sake of our children, I implore each of you to be unyielding and inflexible in your opposition to drugs."[12]
>
> *First Lady Nancy Reagan*

With bi-partisan support, Congress quickly moved on legislation. The Anti-Drug Abuse Act of 1986, featuring mandatory sentencing minimums for drug-related offenses, was passed by Congress.

Upon the law's signing, President Reagan expressed concern for drug users, noting, "We must be intolerant of drugs not because we want to punish drug users but because we care about them and want to help them. This legislation is not intended as a means of filling our jails with drug users."[13]

But jails did in fact soon fill with drug users. And drug-related incarcerations fell hardest on minority communities, despite drugs being similarly prevalent in White communities. That disturbing contradiction remains true today. For many years, death rates from drug overdoses have been highest among White people, yet Black and Hispanic people are far more likely to be imprisoned for drug-related offenses.[d]

Drug abuse is greatest among White people, yet drug-related imprisonments are greatest among Black and Hispanic people.

*Deaths from **drug overdoses** per 100,000 US residents[14]*

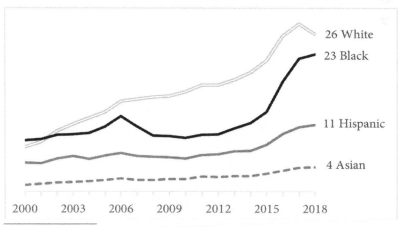

d. For a deeper dive into the intersection of race and criminal justice, see Bryan Stevenson, *Just Mercy: A Story of Justice and Redemption* (New York: Spiegel & Grau, 2015) and Michelle Alexander, *The New Jim Crow: Mass Incarceration in the Age of Colorblindness* (New York: The New Press, 2010).

__Drug-related imprisonments__ per 100,000 US residents (2018)[15]

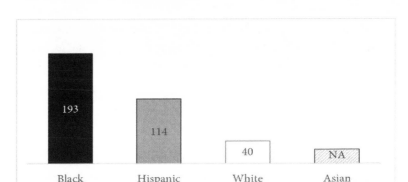

So where does that leave us today? As a nation, where in the long story of race do we now stand? To me, it seems we are stuck in an unsatisfactory place. Legacies of past injustice remain, and attempts to alleviate them can backfire by causing further bitterness. Frustrations, some spoken loudly, and others held privately, abound. And many people struggle to empathize across racial lines. Why? Perhaps because some people know too little about the history of racial injustice, while others know it well and hold a grudge—I have been guilty of each of those. Or maybe people have so isolated themselves in bubbles of like-minded friends that they struggle to understand other perspectives—guilty, again. Whatever the reasons, when reasonable concerns are dismissed as unreasonable gripes, anger is aroused.

During the 2008 presidential campaign, candidate Barack Obama tackled these thorny issues head-on. In a televised address, he pointedly explained,

> ". . . so many of the disparities that exist in the African-American community today can be directly traced to inequalities passed on from an earlier generation that suffered under the brutal legacy of slavery and Jim Crow. Segregated schools were, and are, inferior schools; we

still haven't fixed them, fifty years after *Brown v. Board of Education*, and the inferior education they provided, then and now, helps explain the pervasive achievement gap between today's black and white students. Legalized discrimination—where blacks were prevented, often through violence, from owning property, or loans were not granted to African American business owners, or black homeowners could not access FHA mortgages, or blacks were excluded from unions, or the police force, or fire departments—meant that black families could not amass any meaningful wealth to bequeath to future generations. That history helps explain the wealth and income gap between black and white, and the concentrated pockets of poverty that persists in so many of today's urban and rural communities. A lack of economic opportunity among black men, and the shame and frustration that came from not being able to provide for one's family, contributed to the erosion of black families—a problem that welfare policies for many years may have worsened. And the lack of basic services in so many urban black neighborhoods—parks for kids to play in, police walking the beat, regular garbage pick-up and building code enforcement—all helped create a cycle of violence, blight and neglect that continue to haunt us . . . What's remarkable is not how many failed in the face of discrimination, but rather how many men and women overcame the odds, how many were able to make a way out of no way for those like me who would come after them. But for all those who scratched and clawed their way to get a piece of the American Dream, there were many who didn't make it—those who were ultimately defeated, in one way or another, by discrimination. That legacy of defeat was passed on to future generations—those young men and increasingly young women who we see standing on street corners or languishing in our prisons, without hope or prospects for the future. Even for those blacks who did make it, questions of race, and racism, continue to define their worldview in fundamental ways . . . the memories of humiliation and doubt and fear have not gone away; nor has the anger and the bitterness of those years. That anger may not get expressed in public, in front of white co-workers or white friends. But it does find voice in the barbershop or around the kitchen table. At times, that anger is exploited by politicians, to gin up votes along racial lines, or to make up for a politician's own failings. And occasionally it finds voice in the church on Sunday morning, in the pulpit and in the pews . . . That anger is not always productive; indeed, all too often it distracts attention from solving real problems; it keeps us from squarely facing our own complicity in our condition, and prevents the African-American community from forging the alliances it needs to bring about real change. But the anger is real; it is powerful; and to simply wish it away, to condemn it without understanding its roots, only serves to widen the chasm of misunderstanding that exists between the races."[16]

Barack Obama (as candidate for president)

After voicing these frustrations, Obama immediately transitioned to anger felt by many White people, empathizing with their concerns too. He said,

"In fact, a similar anger exists within segments of the white community. Most working- and middle-class white Americans don't feel that they have been particularly privileged by their race. Their experience is the immigrant experience—as far as they're concerned, no one's handed them anything, they've built it from scratch. They've worked hard all their lives, many times only to see their jobs shipped overseas or their pension dumped after a lifetime of labor. They are anxious about their futures, and feel their dreams slipping away; in an era of stagnant wages and global competition, opportunity comes to be seen as a zero-sum game, in which your dreams come at my expense. So when they are told to bus their children to a school across town; when they hear that an African American is getting an advantage in landing a good job or a spot in a good college because of an injustice that they themselves never committed; when they're told that their fears about crime in urban neighborhoods are somehow prejudiced, resentment builds over time. Like the anger within the black community, these resentments aren't always expressed in polite company. But they have helped shape the political landscape for at least a generation . . . Talk show hosts and conservative commentators built entire careers unmasking bogus claims of racism while dismissing legitimate discussions of racial injustice and inequality as mere political correctness or reverse racism . . . And yet, to wish away the resentments of white Americans, to label them as misguided or even racist, without recognizing they are grounded in legitimate concerns—this too widens the racial divide, and blocks the path to understanding."[17]

Barack Obama (as candidate for president)

Racial division is deep and multi-faceted. On the surface, the divide may not always seem problematic. But hurt and anger, rooted in centuries of injustice and physical and ideological separation, sit just below. These feelings are often kept behind closed doors, but sometimes they erupt in public.

Such was the case in May of 2020 after George Floyd, a Black man, was killed without cause by a White police officer in Minneapolis, Minnesota. Confined to homes due to the COVID-19 pandemic, the nation watched Floyd's death on repeat in news feeds. The simple plea of a dying man, "I can't breathe," was raw. It was human.

In many communities, anger seethed. People took to the streets. Protests formed in all fifty states of the United States and in major cities across the globe. Most demonstrations were peaceful, but some turned violent.

In the weeks following Floyd's death, I attended several large group demonstrations—a protest advocating criminal justice reform, a prayer march, a walk delivering civil rights education, and an event focused on lament. The demographics and ideologies of each event varied considerably. In every case, though, people were moved to action. Across dividing lines of color and creed, most demonstrators were troubled by the status quo, ready to acknowledge racial injustices, and yearning for a more unified future.

As a nation, have we come a long way since the days of slavery? Absolutely, we have. But have we arrived at a destination of racial equity and unity? Not even close. There is a great distance left to travel, disagreement about the target destination, and uncertainty about how best to get there.

This may sound like discouraging news, but I have come to view it differently. The fact that America's journey is unfinished is good news! It means there is hope for better. Moving forward, there are tremendous possibilities. The story of race can have a redeeming conclusion, if only we write one.

CHAPTER 13

Moving Forward

EARLY IN MY studies, as my eyes opened to the legacies of past injustice, I found myself newly disturbed. There were problems, and I wanted to fix them, though I still knew little about them. Fortunately, before leaping into action, I recalled a mistake I often made early in marriage. Whenever my wife shared personal hardships, I would immediately assume the role of a fixer. I just wanted to make her problems go away. My motives were not all bad, but my instincts needed to be retrained. I was slow to realize my wife wants to be heard and understood—not to be fixed. Thankfully, she was patient and persistent, and I gradually learned. Applying that lesson to my study of race, I committed to opening my ears before I opened my mouth, to learning about the roots of division before proposing unifying solutions.

But there is also a time for action. That was another lesson my wife taught. When she opens up about her struggles, especially ones related to our marriage, I should consider tangible ways to help relieve her pain. In our house, love is not passive. Love requires intentionality and hard work. If my concerns are truly genuine, they must move from my head to my hands and feet. Empathetic words spoken on the living room couch must be followed by actions over subsequent days. If necessary, I make sacrifices in my own life in order to improve hers, and she does the same for me.

Likewise, my study of racial division needs to lead to action and, if necessary, personal sacrifice. But what practical steps can I take to push my nation further toward racial equity? That is the question I continually asked myself while writing this book, and it is the question I want to answer in this concluding chapter.

Here, I will not be promoting any political parties or policies, nor will I propose ways you, the reader, can contribute to a better future. My focus is on me. In response to all I have learned, I will vulnerably examine my own life and challenge myself to do better. Which of my self-critiques might also apply to you is for you to decide. The remainder of this book is simply an open letter to myself, written in the third person.

Dear Curtis,

You are deeply flawed. Do not waste time assigning blame or taking solace in being "less flawed" than any other person. The path to a better future begins with you. I encourage you to be brutally honest with yourself and compare who you are today to who you wish to be. The best you can ever hope to be is a work in progress, so you should get to work.

1. Fight Racial Biases

A great place to start would be fighting your own racial biases. Over four decades of life, you have been exposed to a barrage of racial stereotypes, and some of them took residence in your head. Ridding yourself of them will not be easy. You first need to become conscious of your subconscious beliefs. When you meet a new person, you sometimes have instantaneous feelings and unbidden thoughts related to race. They are old habits. You need to recognize, learn to control, and, ultimately, overcome your bias. It will take time.

Biases creep into your thinking in many ways. Sometimes they start as truths and turn into lies. You may learn a fact about one person and assume it holds true for another of the same race. That's bias. Or you may recognize something tends to be true and subconsciously assume it always holds true. For example, based only on race, you could falsely assume a person has below-average income. The truth, of course, is there is a wide range of financial well-being in every racial group. More generally, no group of people thinks alike, votes the same, prefers the same food, and views history in the same way. And no group has the same skill set, knowledge, and financial resources. When you learn an individual's race, the only fact you know is his or her race. Be wary about presuming any additional knowledge based on race alone.

In addition to changing how you think about race, you could also consider letting go of it entirely. You sometimes use race as a descriptor when it is unhelpful. Find opportunities to replace race with more meaningful descriptions. Instead of saying, "Have you met the new school principal? She is Asian," you could say, "Have you met the new school principal? She has worked in education for twenty years and seems really passionate about language arts." In this way, aim to humanize people and elevate them above racial stereotypes.

2. Embrace Diversity

As you continue fighting your racial biases, consider opportunities to embrace greater diversity. Start by recognizing your greatest exposure has always been to White people. Growing up, nearly all your family and friends were White. They are wonderful people! But lack of diversity limited your exposure to other perspectives.

Over the last decade, your circle of friends did grow much more diverse. You opened your eyes to people and social events you previously had not experienced. What was the result? Life became more fun. As you widened your view of the city, it seemed to grow in size and offer more to your family. With a willingness to enter rooms where *you* are the minority, there are now far more adventures you can have and delightful people you can meet.

If you wish to further diversify your circle of friends, some aspect of your basic life structure may need to change. Friendships are naturally built where you spend your time, and most of your time is still spent in predominantly White spaces. Note the racial demographics at the schools, organizations, and other places you frequent. For the most part, they are far Whiter than your city as a whole.

Choosing diversity may require leaving your comfort zone. Instead of asking people to come to you, you could go to them. You could move to a more diverse neighborhood, place your kids in more diverse schools, or find a new church and leisure activities where White people are outnumbered.

3. Keep an Open Mind

As you fight biases and embrace diversity, you will naturally encounter new perspectives on life. Some will be unfamiliar—and may even seem distasteful—but that does not necessarily make them wrong. On any given issue, one view may be right and another view may be wrong, or truth may be in the eye of the beholder.

In adolescence, you naturally learned to see the world like people around you. To some extent, the development of your belief system was like an essay exam in which you were given a blank page and allowed to write whatever you wished, and instead of crafting original beliefs, you took a shortcut and copied a nearby page. Then you treated your copied page as an answer key to grade other people's work. Occasionally, you even gave people failing grades without reading their essays. Perhaps I am being too hard on you, but there is an uncomfortable truth here. Today, though you have grown more receptive to new ideas, you still sometimes blindly dismiss unfamiliar beliefs.

For goodness' sake, you should withhold judgments at least until you understand what you are judging. Place yourself in other people's shoes and learn to see the world as they see it. Push yourself to seek and find the merits of different perspectives. Keep an open mind, particularly on hot-button issues arousing racial tension—such as immigration, criminal justice reform, reparations, minimum wages, income inequality, affirmative action, and entitlement benefits.

4. Speak Up

Keeping an open mind, though, does not require withholding your own opinions. After filling your blank page with original beliefs, you do not have to hide that page in a desk drawer. You are free to post it on a public wall. So when you encounter wrongdoing or have ideas to promote love and justice, speak up!

As you do, there will be some tension. Go ahead and accept that now. Whenever you share an opinion, disagreements are inevitable. For instance, some family members may not approve of the family stories you told in this book. You better grow some thick skin because family disagreements will only be the tip of the iceberg. You may advocate for a tax policy that would financially hurt a friend, endorse a political candidate who seems abhorrent to a neighbor, express concerns about an educational model that a friend passionately supports, and so on. You may argue for broad policies to address past injustices, while other people insist your favored policies are injustices themselves. The bottom line is your idea of helping the world may seem hurtful to other people, and vice versa. Such hurt can be uncomfortable, but it can also be constructive. Remember Martin Luther King Jr.'s warnings against "a negative peace which is the absence of tension." His movement intentionally created "constructive, nonviolent tension which is necessary for growth."

Curtis, heed King's words. You cannot effectively lead if you acquiesce to popular opinion. Stay true to your convictions, even if they require spending lonely nights on ideological islands, isolated from larger groups on the mainland. Remember, unconventional opinions are not necessarily wrong. If you deeply believe in something, then, when opposition comes, place a firm stake in the ground and weather the storm.

But be humble. Your opinions are only opinions, after all. Some of them will be wrong, and others will be impossible to prove right. Furthermore, any wisdom you have is tainted by your many flaws. As you openly share your perspectives, your pride or ignorance may be revealed. Your unconscious biases may become obvious to others before they are apparent to you. And you may communicate poorly, causing people to criticize or misinterpret your message.

When any of those things happen, take a breath, and remember life is not about you. Accept every criticism, including hostile feedback, as a learning opportunity. You can even revisit your opinions after they have been shared. They are not written in stone. When necessary, edit your page of beliefs, and then resume sharing with the world.

5. Live Generously

You have far more to share, however, than just your thoughts. Take an honest look at yourself in the mirror and admit you have more than you need to live comfortably. While many people struggle to get by, you enjoy material excess. Look back over your life and consider how that came to be. If you look from different angles, you will see different truths about your path to prosperity.

From one angle, your comforts appear to be the result of hard work. From grade school through college, you busted your butt in classrooms, sought leadership positions, and stayed out of trouble. You graduated with excellent grades, applied online for an entry-level job, and worked your way up. And you have not inherited a single dollar. Whatever you now have, you earned.

But if you look from another angle, you can see a different truth. In addition to working hard, you also benefited from many privileges, just as your father and grandfather did. As a child, you never lacked for food or feared for your safety. Your home was warm and comfortable. The family doctor was only a phone call away. You learned from two college-educated parents, who supported your own education and paid for every dime. And you were White. Your race promoted self-confidence because you could easily picture yourself joining other White leaders in business, government, or the church. You likely benefitted from favorable treatment, too. In powerful White social circles, you fit in easily. You were an insider in important places where many minorities felt like outsiders. All in all, the circumstances of your upbringing were favorable, and you did not earn them. They were given to you. Are you now willing to give back?

I challenge you to live generously in three ways. First, *be a generous participant in capitalism*. Recognize that every dollar you spend and business decision you make is an exercise of power. Any time you buy the cheapest product knowing its sellers or producers mistreat employees, exploit consumers, or dodge taxes, you are maximizing your own comforts at the expense of the common good. Instead of hoarding power for yourself, use it to benefit others. Commit to earning and spending money in a way that adds value to the world.

Second, *give generously*. Early in your working career, you committed to giving away 10% of your income. To your credit, you stuck by that commitment, which reaped joy. But over time, as your income rose, the joy of giving lessened. Have you considered why that happened? Pardon me for being so blunt, but I believe I know

183

the reason. Your commitment to give away 10% gradually turned into a license to keep 90%. You no longer need to sacrifice much in order to give 10%, and the joy of giving is directly related to the pain of sacrifice. You can give more. And you can more thoughtfully give. It strikes me that a large portion of your current giving comes right back to you. Church tithes, for instance, largely pay for facilities, sermons, and programs serving your own family. I challenge you to consider how much of your current giving goes to people who have far less than you, and aim to give them far more.

Third, *be a generous participant in democracy*. If everyone votes with their own interests in mind, then democracy functions as majority will serving majority interests, potentially at great cost to minority groups. This is a dangerous flaw of an otherwise equitable model of governance. You can counteract that flaw by voting as an altruist, with a driving concern for the well-being of others. There is plenty of room for disagreement between genuine altruists because altruism is not always a clear guide, but it is a better guide than self-interest.

6. Live Graciously

Orienting your life around the interests of other people, rather than yourself, is a nearly impossible task. Moving forward, no matter how hard you try, you will inevitably fail. Sometimes you will hoard power instead of being generous. You will share opinions at the wrong time or in the wrong way, while blindly dismissing other perspectives. You will choose comfort and familiarity over diversity, and racial biases will creep into your words and actions. You may even twist those knives of injustice and draw blood. Over and over again, you will need grace you do not deserve, as will everyone around you. You cannot control how much grace you receive, but you can control how much you give. I urge you to treat people better than they deserve.

When people speak hurtful words, give them the benefit of the doubt instead of rendering immediate judgments. Sometimes words fail everyone. When racial bias is clear and admonishments are required, deliver them in private. You can help people improve themselves without wrecking their reputations.

Similarly, when people make poor decisions, consider their circumstances before making judgments. Their decision-making may be rooted in experiences unfamiliar to you. They may have battled financial, psychological, or social pressures greater than any you have faced.

Extend grace to policymakers as well. They have a tough job. In history books, including this one, they sometimes serve as an easy villain when the blame should really be spread broadly. Policymakers' decisions are also sometimes misunderstood because they face challenges most people do not consider. For instance, rightly or wrongly, a policymaker may believe *increasing* tax rates would inadvertently *decrease* tax revenues by pushing away businesses and wealthy residents. Or she may believe certain types of government assistance are counterproductive because they incentivize negative behaviors. After considering many factors, policymakers sometimes make decisions that belie their ultimate wishes. You can extend grace by assuming their motives are pure, recognizing the complex challenges they face, and debating their policies instead of speculating about their motives.

7. Set High Standards

Lastly, set high standards. Aim for the level of love and justice set forth by your professed role model, Jesus—the man who Martin Luther King Jr. said was "anointed to heal the brokenhearted" and to "deal with the problems of the poor."

Do not measure the state of the nation against past failures; measure it against future possibilities. Envision a day when childhood circumstances and financial outcomes no longer vary by race. There is no good reason such a lofty destination cannot be reached.

Getting there, though, will require taking bold steps. Simply being kind, inclusive, and free of racial bias will not be enough. Direct consequences of past injustices still shape your society, and perpetuation of those consequences is itself an injustice. What are you willing to do to create a more equitable future?

You may need to consider new paths forward, and the best ideas may come from outside the traditional box. So muster the courage to think big.

Remember, the status quo seemed locked in place in the 1960s, yet radical change was on the horizon. Soon after four Black college students started a sit-in protest in your hometown, social norms were remade. Such change was only possible because the protesters refused to be lulled to sleep by the status quo. They kept a wakeful eye on justice, cast bold visions for the future, and hoped for true transformation. Go and do likewise.

Sincerely,
Curtis

Appendix:
Defining Race

AS I JOURNEYED through the story of race, I considered a puzzling question: *What is race?* When the United States was founded, race determined who was granted legal rights to life, liberty, and the pursuit of happiness. Millions of people were enslaved because of their race. Native Americans were pushed aside, Mexicans were not wanted, and Asians were excluded, all because of their race. And the Supreme Court agreed society could be strictly segregated by race. But what *is* race? I needed to grapple with that question.

Still today, the notion of race permeates culture, language, music, bookshelves, news feeds, and political exit polls. It is a key determinant of our social identities. The government includes race as one of just a few identifying markers on official documents. My marriage certificate and driver's license identify my race. Some birth certificates identify parents by race. And race extends beyond written documents to everyday conversations. Racial classifications are commonly used as adjectives to partially describe people, or as nouns to wholly describe them—such as, "Asians are good at math" or "The new mayor is Black." But what *is* race?

It orders social structures. Corporations monitor employee counts by race. Schools report on student populations and performance by race. The corrections system keeps track of prisoner count and frequency of crime by race. But what *is* race? I wanted a definition, not an example.

Seeking answers from self-proclaimed experts, I found passionate disagreements about the significance, and even the existence, of this concept called race. People view race on a spectrum of beliefs. At one end, race is based on genetic distinctions meaningfully influencing social behavior and human abilities. At the other end, race is nothing more than a social construct, an idea existing simply because people created it and then accepted their creation as truth.

For a while, to avoid disagreements about the meaning of race, I tried explaining my book in progress to friends without using any race-related terminology. But avoiding the language of race resulted in awkward and inefficient conversations. I struggled to complete basic sentences like "I am writing a book addressing division based on _____," without inserting the word *race*. As alternatives, I tested the words *color* and *origin*. Neither of those words encompassed the idea of race, and both words confused my audiences. When I reverted to using the word race, people immediately understood the topic. Race is in our language. Race has meaning. Our nation is not divided by color or origin. Our nation is divided by race. But what *is* race?

I looked to the government, the supposed voice of the people, for answers. The Office of Management and Budget last revised the federal guidelines on race in 1997.[1] Its first principle begins, "The racial and ethnic categories set forth in the standards should not be interpreted as being primarily biological or genetic in reference." That makes sense. After all, the study of genetics began long after race had already divided the nation. The first principle continues, "Race and ethnicity may be thought of in terms of social and cultural characteristics as well as ancestry." Or, restating in my own words, "Race has many meanings. It's complicated."

The second principle recommends self-identification, allowing each person to name his or her own race or races. For instance, if one of your parents is Black and the other White, you can identify with either one of those two races, or you can identify with both.

In total, the federal government identifies five major races: (1) White, (2) Black or African American, (3) Asian, (4) Native Hawaiian or Other Pacific Islander, and (5) American Indian or Alaska Native. And then two ethnicities are named: (1) Hispanic, Latino, or Spanish origin and (2) Not Hispanic, Latino, or Spanish origin.

Prior to reading this official guidance, I had not understood race and ethnicity are treated as distinct concepts. Now I notice when they are named separately. On the 2020 census form, for example, I was first asked my ethnicity. I answered Not Hispanic, Latino, or Spanish origin. Then my race was requested, and I checked the box for White.

The federal guidelines addressed a few of my questions, but far more remained unanswered. I still did not have a practical definition of race, not one that could be used in my daily life. My confusions and concerns about race were numerous, but I filtered them down to four major categories.

First and foremost, race is **inconsistently applied**. There is no single right way to determine a person's race. You may be tempted to say you simply "know" it when you see it. Call it a *gut feel*. But the things you presume to know are subjective. Others will disagree, perhaps even take offense.

Suppose you were asked to divide a stadium full of people into separate racial groups, each with its own seating section. How would you proceed? Would you determine each person's race based on physical traits? If so, which traits would be most important—skin color, hair texture, bone structure? How would you treat people whose appearance is blended between two groups? As a tiebreaker, perhaps you would consider culture differences, such as fashion style or food preferences. But can fashions or foods really determine a person's race? And how would you classify people with physical traits associated with one race and cultural characteristics associated with another? Which criterion takes precedence?

There are no official right or wrong answers to practical questions like these. No matter how you assigned the stadium seating, you would encounter opposition because there is no agreeable definition of White. The same goes for Black, Asian, Hispanic, and so on. Answers vary by person, community, and social context. And where clarity is elusive, division is inevitable.

Second, the language of race is **unstable.** Terminology continually changes. I was astounded to learn about the evolution of naming conventions in US censuses.

The first census, taken in 1790, identified every person by location of residence and one of three designations – Free White, Other Free Person, and Slave. That was the entire questionnaire. And for the next fifty years, every census followed similar pattern, simply dividing the population between White and Other, and then Free and Slave.[2]

By 1870, the number of classifications had expanded to five, but they were not yet called *races*; they were called *colors*. White still indicated full European ancestry, Black indicated full African ancestry, and Mulatto signified partial African ancestry, regardless of how small. The final two colors were Chinese and Indian, neither of which has ever appeared in my children's crayon collection. Nevertheless, they were both included in the government's list of colors.[3]

The notion of color was first renamed *race* in the 1890 census, at a time when White Americans were hyper-focused on measuring African ancestry. *Mulatto* became a more exclusive group. Only people with three-eighths to five-eighths "black blood," as it was called then, made the cut. *Quadroon* was added for people with one-fourth black blood, and *Octoroon* for those with one-eighth or less.[4]

Terminology continued changing throughout the 1900s and all the way up to today. *Negro* was added in 1930, and not removed until 2020. *African American* made its first appearance in 2000. Labels for Asian and American Indian people fluctuated as well. Interestingly, the term *Native American*, though commonly used, has never appeared as a race in the census.

The idea of ethnicity was a recent addition. Not until 1970 did a question about Spanish origin appear, and Hispanic and Latino were added later. Still today, there is debate about the meaning of those terms,[a] and some people prefer *Latinx* as a gender-neutral replacement for *Latino/Latina*.

These are just a small sampling of the many ongoing changes in the language of race. In order to speak this language fluently, one must continually set aside outdated words and learn new ones.

Racial classifications are unstable over time.

US Census categories indicating European or African ancestry[5]

Decennial Census Year	Indicators of European Ancestry	Indicators of African Ancestry[b]
1790–1810	Free White	Other Free Person Slave
1820–1840	Free White	Free Colored Slave
1850–1860	White	Black Black Slave Mulatto Mulatto Slave
1870–1880	White	Black Mulatto
1890	White	Black Mulatto Quadroon Octoroon
1900	White	Black

a. *Hispanic* generally relates to Spanish-speaking countries in the Americas, whereas *Latino* is broader, relating to countries and languages with Latin at their root.
b. Now excludes North Africa, which the US Census Bureau groups alongside European and the Middle Eastern ancestry in the White classification.

Decennial Census Year	Indicators of European Ancestry	Indicators of African Ancestry
1910–1920	White	Black Mulatto
1930–1960	White	Negro
1970–1990	White	Black or Negro
2000–2010	White	Black, African American, or Negro
2020	White	Black or African American

Third, racial groupings are **illogical**. How should I explain to my young children the reasoning behind assigning some people color names, such as *White* and *Black*, others geographic names, such as *Asian*, and still others cultural names, such as *Hispanic*? It makes no sense.

The starkness of color-based names was my kids' first introduction to the confusion of race. I fumbled trying to clarify why their elementary school friends, whose skin colors range from light peach to dark brown, are identified as White and Black. And I could not feign any sort of logic explaining why some of their friends with medium-to-light skin color are considered Black.

There are plenty of other examples rooted in ugly history and otherwise devoid of common sense. For instance, it is now acceptable to say "people of color" but certainly not "colored people." And though much of Russia is in the continent of Asia, a person from that region may not be considered Asian. Similarly, the federal government does not consider North Africans, such as people from Egypt, to be African American. Rather, they are counted as White. In yet another point of confusion, many people identify their race as Hispanic even though the government has only considered Hispanic to be an ethnicity, not a race. And the list goes on.

Fourth, and finally, race is **losing relevance**. Cultural and physical distinctions between racial groups are diminishing by the day. They fade as people occupy the same land, sharing the same language, climate, and government. And proximity reduces physical distinctions as well, for the obvious reason that people of every race love sex. Through procreation, separate people groups mix, and dividing lines become irrelevant.

My friend, Daniel, is a great example. His skin color is lighter than his wife's, but much darker than mine. Daniel's mother was a first-generation immigrant from Puerto Rico, with light skin, and his father was born in New York, with medium to dark skin. Like his father, Daniel generally identifies as Black, and he has reason to do so. Several hundred years ago, many of his ancestors did live in Africa. But others lived in Europe and South America. It is possible no single continent was home to a majority of his ancestors.

Daniel and I have become close friends, and have bonded over shared experiences. For several years, we reserved Friday mornings for shared coffee and conversation. We are at similar life stages, both in our late 30s with young kids. Our wives are close friends. Our kids play together. He and his wife host my family for dinner, and we do the same for them because we enjoy being together.

If you were to ask me to identify Daniel's race, how should I respond? Perhaps I would ask what it is you really want to know about him. His physical appearance? Tall, with brown skin tone and short hair. The home of his ancestors? Spread across multiple continents. His beverage preferences? IPA beer and way-too-fancy coffee. Is he kind? Yes, he is one of the kindest men I know. Is he hard-working? Yes, he supports his family by picking up side jobs to supplement his primary income. Does he do good tiling work? No, my home tiling projects are far superior. Can he dance well? Relative to me, everybody can dance well. Is he athletic? Yes, he makes me look foolish on a basketball court. Ask me any clearly defined question about Daniel, and I can give a direct answer. But, his race? I do not know a logical answer, and I often question its relevance.

To recap, the government provides a couple guiding principles for thinking about race, but they fall far short of a practical definition. In my opinion, the very notion of race has four major shortcomings: It is inconsistently applied, unstable, illogical, and losing relevance. Regardless, I still needed a definition of race. So I created one.

Race

Noun: A system used to classify people into groups, with loosely defined ancestral meaning and undefined social and cultural meaning. The way a person's race is determined varies by region and social context.

Adjective: Merely indicates association with a racial group. For instance, a Black person is simply an individual who has been classified as Black, logically or illogically so, and based upon any criteria. As a descriptor, *Black* provides no other concrete information.

Acknowledgments

I AM INDEBTED to so many people for their contributions to this book. Without the emotional support, friendship, vulnerability, candor, subject matter expertise, and sacrifices of others, I could not have produced the work you now hold in your hands. This was a team effort. To those of you on the team, **thank you**!

My wife, Katie Chesney, supported me from beginning to end. Her longing for equity and journey toward self-awareness preceded my own. After I launched into my studies, she kept me stable when I waivered, believed in me when I doubted myself. She also accepted negative financial consequences without hesitation. From the start, this book was my passion project, not my day job. When I proposed cutting my work hours in half to devote myself to research and writing, Katie immediately approved.

My kids—Cooper (12), Annabelle (10), Eliza (8), and Tucker (6)—contributed more than they realize. Sometimes, I worked when they wanted me to play, or I was physically present but mentally absent, distracted by the latest round of manuscript edits. Their innocent questions about race also challenged me to craft simple, yet insightful, answers. I will never forget sitting on my bed with Cooper and Annabelle, reading the entire manuscript aloud.

My parents, Steve and Cathy Chesney, helped in so many ways. Their inflated view of me is as welcome as it is delusional. Words of affirmation is one of my love languages, and they speak it fluently. They also graciously allowed me to write about our family, as did my brother, Luke Chesney, and my sister, Marion Corum.

I also wrote about Chesney families with whom I have no known blood relation, being Pharaoh Chesney and his descendants. David Sharp, one of Pharaoh's living descendants, was incredibly kind and helpful from our very first conversation and continued to touch base with me over the last couple years. Lula Chesney and Almeta Chesney also received me graciously.

Guys in my Be the Bridge group, modeled after an organization whose vision is that people and organizations would be aware and responding to the racial brokenness and systemic injustice in our world, have played an important role in my life over the last few years. Our vulnerable discussions helped me grasp racial nuances that I could never fully gain from a book. Friendship with Dwayne Diaz, who co-founded the group with me, has especially blessed me. The group has also included: David Budler, Sam Cruz, Mark Cummings, Will Dungee, Nate Edmondson, Charlie Heritage, Hunter Oakley, Ronald Redmond, Dale Slaughter, Justin Smith, and Sir Mawn Wilson.

Fellowship over early morning coffee and crepes with Evan Travis and Michael Fulton carried me through up and down times. They were a valuable sounding board as I considered taking on this project.

Most of the people mentioned above reviewed the manuscript. In addition to them, many others also reviewed it, and their willingness to be honest opened my eyes to many blind spots. Both their affirmations and their critiques were beneficial. Reviewers not yet mentioned include: Heather Aherne, Karen Anderson, Craig DeAlmeida, Meeka Diaz, Drew Hill, John Inazu, Kevin James, Seth Kehne, Chavanne Lamb, Bill Lyons, Chad Lynum, Mike Pitts, Suzanne Plihcik, Stephanie Rivers, Matt Vary, Adam Williams, and Sook Yu.

For nearly a decade, my family was part of what we called "small group," a collection of families committed to living life together, listening to one another's joy and pain, and pushing one another toward Jesus. Katie and I deeply value those families. As I set out to write this book, they listened to my hopes and worries and pushed me to keep going. The families included the Heritages, Hills, Smiths, and Whitworths.

Other Voices, a leadership development and community-building experience in which participants build their insight and understanding of the roots of prejudice, challenged me in ways I am still processing today. It was a tremendous experience. I join the other Class of 2020 members in saying we were truly "the best class ever."

The rich community at my church, Grace Community Church of Greensboro, North Carolina, often served as a respite. I have been blessed by the fellowship it provides. The recent and current teaching pastors—Bill Goans, Will Dungee, Marshall Benbow, and Lee Simmons—have continuously challenged me to make disciples who live out the gospel across racial and economic lines. I count all four of them not just as pastors but also as friends.

Extensive copyediting help came from Christi Helms, who refused to accept any payment. Correcting numerous grammar mistakes, she made me sound better than I could sound on my own.

Earlier editing contributions came from Tiffany Acuff. Her frank input set me on a path in the right direction. Despite huge demands on her time, she somehow fit me into her schedule.

Credit for the book cover design and the interior layout goes to Tom Temple and Gretchen Logterman, respectively. They made my work look good, literally. Thank you also to Angela Kerr for taking a great portrait for the back cover.

To help with promotions, many people provided short blurbs attesting to the book's value. To the extent this book garners any interest, much of the credit will go to them.

Lastly, and most importantly, so many subject matter experts provided critical educational resources. Without them, this book simply could not exist. I sat at their feet and soaked in everything I could, which often felt like drinking from a fire hydrant. My idea with this book was not to produce deep insights on a single era or topic, but rather to connect many eras and topics together—like pieces of a puzzle—in a story that was simple, concise, and true. Achieving all three was a daunting task. The experts mentioned in the bibliography were a tremendous help.

I am sincerely thankful for the whole team of people contributing to this work, including those listed and those left out. I owe you one.

Portraits

Chesney, Pharaoh

John Webster, *Last of the Pioneers; or, Old Times in East Tenn.; Being the Life and Reminiscences of Pharaoh Jackson Chesney (aged 120 years)*, (Knoxville: S.B. Newman & Co, 1902).

Douglass, Frederick

George Frances Schreiber, photographer, *Frederick Douglass, head-and-shoulders portrait, facing right*, (April 26, 1870) Photograph, https://www.loc.gov/pictures/item/2004671911/.

Du Bois, William Edward Burghardt (W.E.B.)

Cornelius Marion Battey, photographer, *W.E.B. Du Bois, head-and-shoulders portrait, facing slightly right*, (May 31, 1919), https://www.loc.gov/pictures/item/2003681451/.

Eisenhower, Dwight

Fabian Bachrach, photographer, *Dwight D. Eisenhower, head-and-shoulders portrait, facing slightly left*, (1952) Photograph, https://www.loc.gov/item/96523445/.

Jackson, Andrew

James Barton Longacre, Engraver, *Andrew Jackson / drawn from life and engraved by J.B. Longacre*, (Between 1815 and 1845) Engraving,https://www.loc.gov/item/96523440/.

Jefferson, Thomas

Pendleton's Lithography, and Gilbert Stuart, *Thomas Jefferson, third president of the United States*, United States, ca. 1825, (Boston: Pendleton, on stone by Maurin, to 1828), https://www.loc.gov/item/96523332/.

Johnson, Andrew

Hon. Andrew Johnson, half-length portrait, facing left, (Between 1855 and 1865, printed later)] Photograph, https://www.loc.gov/item/96522530/.

Johnson, Lyndon B.

Lyndon B. Johnson, head-and-shoulders portrait, facing left, (June 1964) Photograph, https://www.loc.gov/item/96522661/.

Kennedy, John F.

President John F. Kennedy, head-and-shoulders portrait, facing front, (1961) Photograph, https://www.loc.gov/item/96523447/.

King, Jr., Martin Luther

Walter Albertin, photographer. *Martin Luther King, Jr., three-quarter-length portrait, standing, facing front, at a press conference,* World Telegram & Sun, (June 8, 1964) Photograph. https://www.loc.gov/item/99404325/.

Lincoln, Abraham

Alexander Gardner, photographer, *Abraham Lincoln, head-and-shoulders portrait, facing front,* ca. 1900, (photograph taken November 8, 1863, printed later) Photograph, https://www.loc.gov/item/96522529/.

Madison, James

Pendleton's Lithography, and Gilbert Stuart, *James Madison, fourth President of the United States,* 1828, Photograph, https://www.loc.gov/item/96522271/.

Obama, Barack

Pete Souza, photographer, *Official portrait of President-elect Barack Obama / Pete Souza,* (2009) Photograph, https://www.loc.gov/item/2010647151/.

Polk, James

President James K. Polk, half-length portrait, seated, facing right. (Between 1855 and 1865, printed later) Photograph, https://www. loc.gov/item/96522397/.

Reagan, Ronald

Ronald Reagan, head-and-shoulders portrait, facing front, (1981) Photograph, https://www.loc.gov/item/96522678/.

Roosevelt, Franklin D.

Elias Goldensky, photographer, *Franklin Delano Roosevelt, head-and-shoulders portrait, facing slightly left,* (December 27, 1933) Photograph, https://www.loc.gov/item/96523441/.

Roosevelt, Theodore

Pach Brothers, photographer, *Theodore Roosevelt, three quarter length portrait, facing front,* (May 11, 1904) Photograph. https:// www.loc.gov/item/2009631526/.

Stephens, Alexander

Brady's National Photographic Portrait Galleries, photographer, *Portrait of Vice President Alexander Stephens, officer of the Confederate States Government,* (Between 1860 and 1865) Photograph, https://www.loc.gov/item/2018666528/.

Washington, Booker T.

Frances Benjamin Johnston, photographer, *Booker T. Washington, half-length portrait, seated,* (1895) Photograph, https:// www.loc.gov/item/2010645746/.

X, Malcolm

Herman Hiller, photographer, *Malcolm X at Queens Court,* World Telegram & Sun, (1964) Photograph, https://www.loc.gov/ item/97519439/.

Bibliography

Alexander, Michelle. *The New Jim Crow: Mass Incarceration in the Age of Colorblindness, Revised Edition*. New York: The New Press, 2012.

Allen, Robert C. *Global Economic History: A Very Short Introduction*. New York: Oxford University Press, 2011.

Angelou, Maya. *I Know Why the Caged Bird Sings*. New York: Random House, 1969.

Baldwin, James. *The Fire Next Time*. New York: The Dial Press, 1963.

Baptist, Edward E. *The Half Has Never Been Told: Slavery and the Making of American Capitalism*. New York: Basic Books, 2014.

Baradaran, Mehrsa. *The Color of Money: Black Banks and the Racial Wealth Gap*. Cambridge: The Belknap Press of Harvard, 2017.

Barnes, Melody, host, and PRX. "Season Two: LBJ and the Great Society." *LBJ and the Great Society*. Podcast audio, 2020.

Blight, David. *HIST 119: The Civil War and Reconstruction Era, 1845-1877*. Open Yale Courses. Podcast audio, lecture series, Spring 2008.

Bonilla-Silva, Eduardo. *Racism without Racists: Color-blind Racism and the Persistence of Racial Inequality in America*. Fifth Edition. Lanham: Rowman & Littlefield, 2018.

Brown, Austin Channing. *I'm Still Here: Black Dignity in a World Made for Whiteness*. New York: Convergent, 2018.

Carson, Clayborne. *The Autobiography of Martin Luther King, Jr.* New York: Grand Central Publishing, 1998.

Coates, Ta-Nehisi. *Between the World and Me*. New York: Spiegel & Grau, 2015.

Cogan, John F. *The High Cost of Good Intentions: A History of U.S. Federal Entitlement Programs*. Stanford: Stanford University Press, 2017.

Douglass, Frederick. *Narrative of the Life of Frederick Douglass, an American Slave*. Boston: The Anti-Slavery Office, 1845.

Du Bois, William Edward Burghardt (W.E.B.). *The Souls of Black Folk*. Chicago: A.C. McClurg and Co., 1903.

Durand, John D. *Historical Estimates of World Population: An Evaluation*. Philadelphia: University of Pennsylvania, 1974.

Dyson, Michael Eric. *Tears We Cannot Stop: A Sermon to White America*. New York: St. Martin's Press, 2017.

Gates Jr., Henry Louis, writer and presenter. *Looking for Lincoln*. Kunhardt-McGee Productions, Inkwell Films and THIRTEEN for WNET.ORG in association with Ark Media, 2009.

Gerber, David A. *American Immigration: A Very Short Introduction*. New York: Oxford University Press, 2011.

Gonzalez, David James, host, with guest Miriam Pawel. "The Crusades of Cesar Chavez." *New Books in Latin American Studies*. Podcast audio, 2015.

Gonzalez, Juan. *Harvest of Empire: A History of Latinos in America, Revised Edition*. New York: Penguin Group, 2011.

Graham, Lindsay, host. "Season 1: The Cold War." *American History Tellers*, a Wondery production. Podcast audio, 2018.

Haley, Alex. *Roots*. Garden City: Doubleday & Company, 1976.

Hilfiker, David. *Urban Injustice: How Ghettos Happen*. New York: Seven Stories Press, 2002.

Hillier, Amy E. "Who Received Loans? Home Owners' Loan Corporation Lending and Discrimination in Philadelphia in the 1930s." *Journal of Planning History*, no. 1 (February 2003): 3–24.

Hsu, Madeline Y. *Asian American History: A Very Short Introduction.* New York: Oxford University Press, 2017.

Inazu, John D. *Confident Pluralism: Surviving and Thriving through Deep Difference.* Chicago: The University of Chicago Press, 2016.

Irving, Debbie. *Waking up White, and Finding Myself in the Story of Race.* Cambridge: Elephant Room Press, 2014.

Kennedy, John F. *A Nation of Immigrants.* New York: Harper & Row, 1964.

Lee, Erika. *The Making of Asian America: A History.* New York: Simon & Schuster, 2015.

Lepore, Jill. *These Truths: A History of the United States.* New York: W.W. Norton & Company, 2018.

Lynum, Kara, host, and Studio Americana. "Season 1 and Season 2. Immigration Nation." Podcast audio, 2018.

Manson, Steven, and Jonathan Schroeder, David Van Riper, and Steven Ruggles. IPUMS National Historical Geographic Information System: Version 14.0 [Database]. Minneapolis: IPUMS, 2019. http://doi.org/10.18128/D050.V14.0.

Mukherjee, Siddhartha. *The Gene: An Intimate History.* New York: Simon & Schuster, 2016.

National Advisory Commission on Civil Disorders, sometimes called the Kerner Commission. *Report of the National Advisory Commission on Civil Disorders.* New York: Bantam Books, 1968.

National Center for Education Statistics. *120 Years of American Education: A Statistical Portrait.* By Thomas Snyder. Hyattsville, 1993.

Newbell, Trillia J. United: *Captured by God's Vision for Diversity.* Chicago: Moody Publishers, 2014.

Office of Management and Budget. *Historical Tables.* https://www.whitehouse.gov/omb/historical-tables/.

Office of Management and Budget. "Revisions to the Standards for the Classification of Federal Data on Race and Ethnicity." *Federal Register* 62, no. 210 (October 30, 1997): 5872–5890. https://www.govinfo.gov/content/pkg/FR-1997-10-30/pdf/97-28653.pdf

Perkins, John. *One Blood: Parting Words to the Church on Race and Love.* Chicago: Moody Publishers, 2018.

Peters, Gerhard Peters and John T. Woolley. The American Presidency Project. https://www.presidency.ucsb.edu.

Pew Research Center. "What the Census Calls Us." Last updated February 6, 2020. https://www.pewresearch.org/interactives/what-census-calls-us

Robinson, Natasha Sistrunk. *A Sojourner's Truth: Choosing Freedom and Courage in a Divided World.* Downers Grove: IVP Books, 2018.

Rothstein, Richard. *The Color of Law: A Forgotten History of How Our Government Segregated America.* New York: Liveright Publishing Corporation, 2017.

Rutherford, Adam. *A Brief History of Everyone Who Ever Lived: The Human Story Retold Through Our Genes.* New York: The Experiment, 2017.

Saez, Emmanuel, and Gabriel Zucman. *The Triumph of Injustice: How the Rich Dodge Taxes and How to Make Them Pay.* New York: W.W. Norton & Company, 2019.

Sigward, Daniel. *The Reconstruction Era and The Fragility of Democracy.* 2015. https://www.facinghistory.org/.

Slave Voyages, Trans-Atlantic Slave Trade Database, accessed July 2020, https://www.slavevoyages.org/voyage/database.

Stevenson, Bryan. *Just Mercy: A Story of Justice and Redemption.* New York: Spiegel & Grau, 2015.

Stowe, Harriet Beecher. *Uncle Tom's Cabin; or, Life among the Lowly.* Boston: John P. Jewitt & Company, 1852.

Suarez, Ray. *Latino Americans: The 500-Year Legacy That Shaped a Nation.* New York: Celebra, 2013.

Tatum, Beverly Daniel. *Why Are All the Black Kids Sitting Together in the Cafeteria?* New York: Basic Books, 1997.

Tisby, Jemar. *The Color of Compromise: The Truth about the American Church's Complicity in Racism.* Grand Rapids: Zondervan, 2019.

United Nations Population Division. *The World at Six Billion.* October 1999.

United States Census Bureau. *Historical Income Tables: Families.* https://www.census.gov/data/tables/time-series/demo/income-poverty/historical-income-families.html.

United States Census Bureau. "Through the Decades: Index of Questions." https://www.census.gov/history/www/through_the_decades/index_of_questions/.

United States Department of Education, National Center for Health Education Statistics. "The Condition of Education 2018 (NCES 2018-144)." May 2018.

United States Department of Education, National Center for Health Education Statistics. "120 Years of American Education: A Statistical Portrait." January 1993.

United States Department of Homeland Security, Office of Immigration Statistics. "Annual Report: Lawful Permanent Residents." August 2018.

United States Department of Homeland Security, Office of Immigration Statistics. "Illegal Alien Population Residing in the United States: January 2015." December 2018.

United States Library of Congress. Congressional Research Service. *Drug Enforcement in the United States: History, Policy, and Trends.* By Lisa Sacco. R43749, 2014.

United States Library of Congress. Congressional Research Service. *Federal Spending on Benefits and Services for People with Low*

Income: In Brief. By Gene Falk, Karen Lynch, and Jessica Tollestrup. R45097, 2018.

United States Library of Congress. Congressional Research Service. *FHA-Insured Home Loans: An Overview.* By Katie Jones. RS20530, 2018.

United States Library of Congress. Congressional Research Service. *Poverty and Economic Opportunity.* By Gene Falk, Maggie McCarty and Joseph Dalaker. IF10562, 2016.

Wade, Nicholas. *A Troublesome Inheritance: Genes, Race and Human History.* New York: Penguin Group, 2015.

Washington, Booker T. *Up from Slavery.* New York: Doubleday, Page and Company, 1901.

Webster, John Coram. *Last of the Pioneers; or, Old Times in East Tenn.; Being the Life and Reminiscences of Pharaoh Jackson Chesney (aged 120 Years).* Knoxville: S.B. Newman & Co., 1902.

Wells-Barnett, Ida B. *The Red Record.* Independently Published, 1895.

Woodward, Vann C. *The Strange Career of Jim Crow, Third Revised Edition.* New York: Oxford University Press, 1974.

Wright, Carroll D. *The History and Growth of the United States Census: Prepared for the Senate Committee on the Census.* Washington: Government Printing Office, 1900.

X, Malcolm, and Alex Haley. *The Autobiography of Malcolm X.* New York: Grove Press, 1965.

Endnotes

Introduction: Waking to Division

1. Data for 2020 is not yet available, so the map uses data from the 2017 American Community Survey (ACS) as a proxy for 2020. ACS data was provided by: Steven Manson, Jonathan Schroeder, David Van Riper, and Steven Ruggles, IPUMS National Historical Geographic Information System: Version 13.0 [Database], (Minneapolis: University of Minnesota, 2018). http://doi.org/10.18128/D050. V13.0. Hereafter, this data source is abbreviated as IPUMS NHGIS.

2. Reflects an estimate as of July 1, 2019, as provided by: "QuickFacts," US Census Bureau, accessed August 31, 2020, https://www.census.gov/quickfacts.

3. *Historical Income Tables*, "Table F-5. Race and Hispanic Origin of Householder— Families by Median and Mean Income," US Census Bureau, https://www.census. gov/data/tables/time-series/demo/income-poverty/historical-income-families. html.

Chapter 1: Changing Over Time

1. I am unaware of any birth records for Pharaoh. Immediately following his death in 1902, newspapers in at least 10 different states reported he had died at age 126. Without offering proof, most of them cited an exact day of birth of July 4, 1776. Newspapers reporting his death included:

    The Knoxville Sentinel, Knoxville, TN (July 9, 1902).

    Evening Times-Republican, Marshalltown, IA (July 10, 1902).

    The News and Herald, Winnsboro, SC (July 16, 1902).

    Belding Banner, Belding, MI (July 17, 1902).

    The Goldsboro Headlight, Goldsboro, NC (July 17, 1902).

    The Columbia Herald, Columbia, TN (July 18, 1902).

    Windham County Reformer, Brattleboro, VT (July 18, 1902).

    The Gazette, Cleveland, OH (July 19, 1902).

    The Colored American, Washington, D.C. (August 2, 1902).

    The St. Paul Globe, St. Paul, MN (August 25, 1902).

    The Weekly Sentinel, Fort Wayne, IN (January 28, 1903).

    The Opelousas Courier, St. Landry, LA (May 16, 1903).

2. National Human Genome Research Institute, "Genetics vs. Genomics Factsheet," last modified September 7, 2018, https://www.genome.gov/about-genomics/fact-sheets/Genetics-vs-Genomics/.

Chapter 2: Declaring Liberty for Some

1. John Durand, "Historical Estimates of World Population: An Evaluation," *PSC Analytical and Technical Report Series 9*, (1974): 53–60. Also, Alan Taylor, *American Colonies: The Settling of North America* (New York: Penguin, 2001), 40.
2. Today, there is a wide range of naming conventions for this people group. Many prefer to be called by their tribal names, such as Cherokee. Some prefer the term *Indian* and others prefer *Native American*, or simply *Native*. In the 2020 Census and other federal surveys, *American Indian or Alaska Native* is one of five primary racial groups in America. In this book, the terms *American Indian* and *Natives* are used interchangeably, despite their shortcomings.
3. Durand, "Historical Estimates of World Population," 53–60.
4. Trans-Atlantic Slave Trade Database, Voyages, accessed August 31, 2020, https://www.slavevoyages.org/assessment/estimates.
5. Trans-Atlantic Slave Trade Database, Voyages.
6. Julian P. Boyd (editor), *The Papers of Thomas Jefferson: Volume 1, 1760–1776*, (Princeton: Princeton University Press, 1950), 243–47, accessed August 31, 2020, https://www.loc.gov/exhibits/declara/ruffdrft.html.

Chapter 3: Building a White Nation

1. James Madison, *Notes of Debates in the Federal Convention of 1787*, notes from the day of June 30, 1787.
2. Trans-Atlantic Slave Trade Database, Voyages.
3. Data source for chart: US Census Bureau data provided by IPUMS NHGIS.
4. Calculated from the 1790 Census provided by IPUMS NHGIS.
5. An Act to establish an uniform Rule of Naturalization, US Statutes at Large 1 (1790): 103.
6. Andrew Jackson, "Fifth Annual Message," December 3, 1833, Online by Gerhard Peters and John T. Woolley, The American Presidency Project, accessed August 31, 2020, https://www.presidency.ucsb.edu/node/200846.
7. Constitution of the Republic of Texas, General Provisions, Section 9 (1836), accessed August 31, 2020, https://tarltonapps.law.utexas.edu/constitutions/texas1836/general_provisions.
8. Abraham Lincoln, *Abraham Lincoln papers: Abraham Lincoln to Congress, Speech regarding Mexican War*, January 12, 1848, https://www.loc.gov/item/mal0007400/.
9. John Calhoun, speaking on the Conquest of Mexico, 30th Congress, 1st session, Appendix to the Congressional Globe (January 4, 1848): 49-53.
10. Data source for US portion of the map: 1830 Census data provided by IPUMS NHGIS. Mexican territory was manually shaded based on inspection of an 1830 map provided by email by the Institute of Geography of the UNAM (National Autonomous University of Mexico).

Chapter 4: Splintering in Two

1. "Index of Questions: 1850," US Census Bureau, https://www.census.gov/history/www/through_the_decades/index_of_questions/1850_1.html.
2. This section about Pharaoh is based on general information contained in: John Webster, *Last of the Pioneers; or, Old Times in East Tenn.; Being the Life and Reminiscences of Pharaoh Jackson Chesney (aged 120 years)* (Knoxville: S.B. Newman & Co, 1902).
3. Webster, *Last of the Pioneers*, 26.
4. *An Act to divorce John Chesney from his wife Sarah Chesney*, 1883, State of Tennessee, 20th General Assembly, 1st session.
5. Webster, *Last of the Pioneers*, 128.
6. Excerpt from a September 18, 1858 debate between Abraham Lincoln and Stephen Douglass, as recorded in: Mark Neely Jr., *The Abraham Lincoln Encyclopedia* (New York: Da Capo Press, Inc, 1984).
7. Frederick Douglass, *Oration by Frederick Douglass Delivered on the Occasion of the Unveiling of the Freedmen's Monument Memory of Abraham Lincoln* (Washington, D.C.: Gibson Brothers, 1876), 10, https://www.loc.gov/item/mfd.23004/.
8. Population percentages in the footnote were calculated from 1860 Census data provided by IPUMS NHGIS.
9. State of South Carolina, *Declaration of the Immediate Causes Which Induce and Justify the Secession of South Carolina from the Federal Union* (December 24, 1860), accessed August 31, 2020, http://avalon.law.yale.edu/19th_century/csa_scarsec.asp.
10. State of Mississippi, *Proceedings of the Mississippi State Convention* (January 26, 1861), accessed August 31, 2020, https://docsouth.unc.edu/imls/missconv/missconv.html.
11. State of Georgia, *Journal of the Public and Secret Proceedings of the Convention of the People of Georgia* (January 29, 1861), 109, accessed August 31, 2020, https://docsouth.unc.edu/imls/georgia/georgia.html.
12. State of Texas, *A Declaration of the Causes which Impel the State of Texas to Secede from the Federal Union* (February 2, 1861), accessed August 31, 2020, http://avalon.law.yale.edu/19th_century/csa_texsec.asp.
13. Confederate States of America, *Provisional and Permanent Constitutions, of the Confederate States* (Richmond: Tyler, Wise, Allegre and Smith, Printers, 1861), 21, accessed August 31, 2020, https://docsouth.unc.edu/imls/confconstitution/const.html.
14. All data points were calculated from decennial US census data provided by IPUMS NHGIS.
15. Edward Baptist, *The Half Has Never Been Told* (New York: Basic Books, 2014), 114.
16. Data source for chart: 1850 and 1860 US Census provided by IPUMS NHGIS.
17. Data source for chart: 1860 US Census provided by IPUMS NHGIS.
18. Data source for map: 1860 US Census provided by IPUMS NHGIS.

Chapter 5: Beginning Liberty for All

1. Abraham Lincoln, *Copy of Lincoln's second inaugural address as it appears on the North wall of the Lincoln memorial, Washington, D. C. National Park service* (Washington: 1942), https://www.loc.gov/item/rbpe.24203400/.

2. Edmund Kirke, "Our Visit to Richmond," *The Atlantic*, (September 1864).

3. Wanda Wilmouth Underwood, "John Chesney, Solider, War of 1812," *Union County Pathways*, Volume 3, No. 1, (January–March 1984): 8–9.

4. Underwood, "John Chesney, Soldier, War of 1812."

5. Abraham Lincoln, "A Letter from the President to Hon. Horace Greeley," *Daily National Intelligencer*, April 23, 1862, https://www.loc.gov/item/mal4233400/.

6. Elsie Freeman, Wynell Burroughs Schamel, and Jean West, "The Fight for Equal Rights: A Recruiting Poster for Black Soldiers in the Civil War," *Social Education* 56, 2 (February 1992): 118–20, as provided by the National Archives, accessed August 31, 2020, https://www.archives.gov/education/lessons/blacks-civil-war.

7. There is a broad range of estimates for total Civil War deaths, reaching about five hundred thousand at the low end. Estimates above six hundred thousand are more commonly cited, and some experts believe the count was even higher. Here is a recent study estimating 750,000 deaths: David Hacker, "A Census-Based Count of the Civil War Dead," *Civil War History*, Volume 57, No. 4 (December 2011).

8. From 1860 to 1870, the total "true value of real and personal estate" increased 94% across the states remaining in the Union while decreasing 47% across states of the Confederacy. Data calculated from 1860 Census and 1870 Census results provided by IPUMS NHGIS.

9. Henry Cleveland, *Alexander H. Stephens, in Public and Private: With Letters and Speeches, Before, During, and Since the War* (Philadelphia, 1886), 721.

10. "Vetoes, 1789 to Present," United States Senate, accessed August 31, 2020, https://www.senate.gov/legislative/vetoes/vetoCounts.htm.

11. As of 1860, there were 4.0 million slaves and 395,216 slaveholders. Calculated from the 1860 Census provided by IPUMS NHGIS.

12. Daniel Sigward, *The Reconstruction Era and The Fragility of Democracy* (Facing History and Ourselves, 2015), 130–31. For more information, visit www.facinghistory.org.

13. Frederick Douglass, *Life and Times of Frederick Douglass* (Boston: De Wolfe & Fiske Co., 1892), 444, as provided by UNC at Chapel Hill, accessed August 31, 2020, https://docsouth.unc.edu/neh/dougl92/dougl92.html.

14. "Transcript, Meeting between President Andrew Johnson and a Delegation of African-Americans, White House, February 7, 1866," House Divided: The Civil War Research Engine at Dickinson College, accessed August 31, 2020, http://hd.housedivided.dickinson.edu/node/45144.

15. Transcript, Meeting between President Andrew Johnson and a Delegation of African-Americans.

16. Douglass, *Life and Times*, 468.

17. Andrew Johnson, "Third Annual Message Online by Gerhard Peters and John T. Woolley," The American Presidency Project, accessed August 31, 2020, https://www.presidency.ucsb.edu/node/201999.

18. "Demographics of members of Congress," *Vital Statistics on Congress*, The Brookings Institution, last updated March 2019, https://www.brookings.edu/multi-chapter-report/vital-statistics-on-congress/.

19. "Presidential Election of 1868: A Resource Guide," The Library of Congress, accessed August 31, 2020, https://www.loc.gov/rr/program/bib/elections/election1868.html.

20. Distribution of total real estate and personal property: 99.4% held by White residents, 0.5% by Black residents, and a small remainder by Chinese or American Indian residents. Average value of real estate and personal property per person, by race: White $747, Black $27. Calculated from the 1% data sample of the 1870 Census provided by IPUMS NHGIS.

21. Childhood school enrollment reflects ages 7–15. Adult literacy reflects ages 21+. Calculated from the 1% data sample of the 1870 Census provided by IPUMS NHGIS.

22. Calculated from the 1% data sample of the 1870 Census provided by IPUMS NHGIS.

Chapter 6: Excluding Outsiders

1. Underwood, "John Chesney, Solider, War of 1812." The article misspelled Pharoah as "Pharoah." To avoid confusion, I altered the quote to show the proper spelling of his name.

2. Based on my review of the Union County Records of Deeds housed at the Calvin M. McClung Historical Collection in Knoxville, TN.

3. Based on my review of the Union County Records of Deeds housed at the Calvin M. McClung Historical Collection in Knoxville, TN.

4. "Collection Grows Toward Pharaoh Chesney Day," Knoxville News-Sentinel, August 21, 1983, F11.

5. "Key Questions," Chinese Railroad Workers in North America Project at Stanford University, accessed August 31, 2020, https://web.stanford.edu/group/chineserailroad/cgi-bin/website/faqs/.

6. Childhood school enrollment reflects ages 7–15. Adult literacy reflects ages 21+. Calculated from the 1% data samples of the 1870 Census and 1900 Census provided by IPUMS NHGIS.

7. Wealth figures reflect the "true valuation of real and personal estate" in the 1870 Census, filtered to males age 21 and older; minimal wealth was held by females and people under age 21. Reference to people having "zero wealth" includes all people with less than $250 of wealth. The 1870 census was used here because questions on wealth were excluded from censuses in 1880, 1890, and 1900. All calculations were based on the 1% data sample of the 1870 Census provided by IPUMS NHGIS.

8. Lee Ann Potter and Wynell Schamel, "The Homestead Act of 1862," *Social Education* 61, 6 (October 1997): 359–364.

9. *Historical Statistics of the United States, Colonial Times to 1957, Bureau of the Census* (Washington D.C.: US Government Printing Office, 1960), Series K 298–306, K 265–273, and K 83–97.

10. *2018 Yearbook of Immigration Statistics*, "Table 1. Persons Obtaining Lawful Permanent Resident Status: Fiscal years 1820 to 2018," US Department of Homeland Security, accessed August 31, 2020, https://www.dhs.gov/immigration-statistics/yearbook/2018/table1.

11. Constitution of the State of California, Article 19, Sections 2–3, 1879.

12. *In Re Ah Yup*, Case No. 104, Circuit Court, D. California, April 29, 1878.

13. John F. Miller, speaking on S. No. 71, 47th Congress, 1st session, Congressional Record 13 (February 28, 1882): S 1481–88.

14. Miller, speaking on S. No. 71.

15. Miller, speaking on S. No. 71.
16. RJ Ramey (Editor), *Monroe Work Today Dataset Compilation (version 1)*, "Lynching, Whites and Negroes, 1882-1968," Archives of Tuskegee University, Tuskegee, AL, http://archive.tuskegee.edu/archive/handle/123456789/511.
17. An act to protect all citizens in their civil and legal rights, US Statutes at Large 43 (1875): 335-37.
18. Civil Rights Cases, 109 US 3, 24 (1883).
19. *Plessy v. Ferguson*, 163 US 537, 537 (1896).
20. *Plessy v. Ferguson*, 163 US 537, 548-51 (1896).
21. *Plessy v. Ferguson*, 163 US 537, 557-63 (1896).
22. Booker T. Washington, *Up From Slavery* (New York: Doubleday & Company, 1900, 1901), 39, https://docsouth.unc.edu/fpn/washington/washing.html.
23. Washington, *Up From Slavery*, 282, 318.
24. Washington, *Up From Slavery*, 221-22.

Chapter 7: Entrenching Bias

1. John Webster, *Last of the Pioneers; or, Old Times in East Tenn.; Being the Life and Reminiscences of Pharaoh Jackson Chesney (aged 120 years)* (Knoxville: S.B. Newman & Co, 1902), 27.
2. Gardiner Harris, "The Underside of the Welcome Mat," *The New York Times*, November 8, 2008.
3. *The Times-Democrat*, (New Orleans, LA), October 18, 1901, 4.
4. *The Yorkville Enquirer*, (Yorkville, SC), October 30, 1901, 2.
5. Ed Issa, "Indy held spotlight 70 years ago," *The Delta Democrat-Times* (Greenville, MS), October 3, 1972, 24.
6. Originally printed in the Missouri Sedalia Sentinel with an unnamed author and then reprinted in many other newspapers, such as: "Niggers in the White House," *The Windsor Review*, (Windsor, MO), October 31, 1901, 2.
7. Booker T. Washington, *My Larger Education* (New York: Doubleday, Page & Company, 1911), 178-80, https://docsouth.unc.edu/fpn/washeducation/washing.html.
8. W.E. Burghardt Du Bois, *The Souls of Black Folk* (Chicago: A.C. McClurg & Co., 1903), 31, https://docsouth.unc.edu/church/duboissouls/dubois.html.
9. Du Bois, *Souls*, 56.
10. Du Bois, *Souls*, 52, 177.
11. Du Bois, *Souls*, 52, 183-84.
12. Du Bois, *Souls*, 58-59.
13. Donald MacKenzie, "Eugenics in Britain," *Social Studies of Science* Vol. 6 (1976), 514.
14. Only Ethiopia and Liberia retained their independence. All other territory was claimed in some way by European empires.
15. "The Immigration Act of 1924 (The Johnson-Reed Act)," US Department of State, Office of the Historian, accessed August 31, 2020, https://history.state.gov/milestones/1921-1936/immigration-act.
16. *Statistical Abstract of the United States:1999*, "Table No. 1416. Immigration, by Leading Country or Region of Last Residence: 1901 to 1997," US Census Bureau (1999).
17. *Vital Statistics on Congress*, The Brookings Institution.

18. "Offers 'Niggers' Poem," *The Evening Tribune*, (Providence, RI), June 18, 1929, 7.

19. Calculated from OCC1950 codes applied to the 1930 Census, as provided by IPUMS NHGIS.

20. Percent of US Congress: *Vital Statistics on Congress*, The Brookings Institution Life Expectancy at Birth: *Health, United States, 2018 – Data Finder*, "Table 4: Life expectancy at birth, at age 65, and at age 75, by sex, race, and Hispanic origin: United States, selected years 1900–2017," National Center for Health Statistics, (Hyattsville, Maryland: 2019), accessed August 31, 2020, https://www.cdc.gov/nchs/hus/contents2018.htm. All other data in the chart: Calculated from 1% data samples of the 1870, 1900, and 1930 Censuses, provided by IPUMS NHGIS. Labor force in agriculture represents industry code #105 based on the 1950 labor force code categorization.

21. Data source for chart: *Vital Statistics on Congress*, The Brookings Institution.

Chapter 8: Segregating Threats

1. The Dow Jones Industrial Stock Price Index dropped 87% from 9/1/1929 to 6/1/1932.

2. Thomas Piketty and Emmanuel Saez, Income Inequality in the United States, 1913-2002, "Table A3: Top fractiles income shares (including capital gains) in the U.S.," (November 2004): 69, accessed on August 31, 2020, https://eml.berkeley.edu/~saez/piketty-saezOUP04US.pdf.

3. Represents people aged 25–29 (as of the year 1940) who had completed at least four years of college. *CPS Historical Time Series Tables*, "Table A-2: Percent of People 25 Years and Over Who Have Completed High School or College, by Race, Hispanic Origin and Sex: Selected Years 1940 to 2019," US Census Bureau, last revised March 9, 2020, https://www.census.gov/data/tables/time-series/demo/educational-attainment/cps-historical-time-series.html.

4. Represents people aged 25–29 (as of the year 1940) who had completed at least four years of high school. *CPS Historical Time Series Tables*, "Table A-2," US Census Bureau.

5. 1940 Census, Knox County, TN, Civil District 13, Sheet 1B, Enumeration District 47–33.

6. Huey Long, "Speech to Senate Staffers at the Washington Press Club," accessed August 31, 2020, https://www.americanrhetoric.com/speeches/hueyplongbarbe-cuespeechpressclub.htm.

7. "Share Our Wealth," Long Legacy Project, accessed August 31, 2020, https://www.hueylong.com/programs/share-our-wealth.php.

8. US Library of Congress, Congressional Research Service, *FHA-Insured Home Loans: An Overview*, by Katie Jones, RS20530 (2018), 1.

9. *Underwriting Manual*, Federal Housing Authority, (Washington, D.C: US Government Printing Office, 1936).

10. *Underwriting Manual*, Federal Housing Authority.

11. *Underwriting Manual*, Federal Housing Authority.

12. Larry DeWitt, "The Decision to Exclude Agricultural and Domestic Workers from the 1935 Social Security Act," *Social Security Bulletin* 70, no. 4, 2010.

13. California Senate, *An act to add Chapter 8.5 (commencing with Section 8720) to Division 1 of Title 2 of the Government Code, relating to Mexican repatriation,* Senate Bill No. 670, Chapter 663, October 7, 2005.

14. John DeWitt, testimony before a subcommittee of the House Naval Affairs Committee, "Gen. John L. DeWitt Personal Papers – Records Relating to Military Service, 1921–1946," April 13, 1943.

15. *An Act to implement recommendations of the Commission on Wartime Relocation and Internment of Civilians,* Public Law 100-383, US Statutes at Large 102 (1988): 903.

16. Paul's seven cent hourly wage is based upon his total labor hours and total pay reported in the 1940 Census. Similar info from the 1950 Census was not available. 1940 Census, Knox County, TN, Civil District 13, Sheet 1B, Enumeration District 47–33.

17. *Data Finder*, "Table 4: Life expectancy at birth," National Center for Health Statistics.

18. Thomas Snyder, *120 Years of American Education: A Statistical Portrait*, "Table 6. – Percentage of persons 14 years old and over who were illiterate, by race and nativity: 1870 to 1979," National Center for Education Statistics, US Department of Education, (1993): 21.

19. *Historical Income Tables*, "Table F-6: Regions--Families (All Races) by Median and Mean Income," US Census Bureau.

20. *Shelley v. Kraemer*, (1948)

21. Harry Truman, "Executive Order 9981: Establishing the President's Committee on Equality of Treatment and Opportunity in the Armed Services," July 26, 1948, Harry S. Truman Library & Museum, accessed August 31, 2020, https://www.trumanlibrary.gov/library/executive-orders/9981/executive-order-9981.

Chapter 9: Conceding Civility

1. *To Secure These Rights: The Report of the President's Committee on Civil Rights,* Committee on Civil Rights, (Washington, D.C.: US Government Printing Office, 1947), 100 and 147.

2. *Brown v. Board of Education of Topeka et al,* 347 US 483 (1954).

3. Cabell Phillips, "Up Front In The Battle of Central High," *The Gazette and Daily* (York, PA), November 9, 1962, 23.

4. Michael O'Donnell, "Commander v. Chief: The lessons of Eisenhower's civil-rights struggle with his chief justice Earl Warren," *The Atlantic*, (April 2018).

5. Dwight D. Eisenhower, "Radio and Television Address to the American People on the Situation in Little Rock," September 24, 1957, Online by Gerhard Peters and John T. Woolley, The American Presidency Project, https://www.presidency.ucsb.edu/node/233623.

6. Clayborne Carson, editor, *The Autobiography of Martin Luther King, Jr.* (New York: Grant Central Publishing, 1998), 351.

7. Martin Luther King Jr., "Letter from Birmingham Jail," April 16, 1963, as provided by The Martin Luther King Jr. Research and Education Institute of Stanford University.

8. King, "Letter from Birmingham Jail."

9. King, "Letter from Birmingham Jail."

10. Beverly Gage, "What an Uncensored Letter to M.L.K. Reveals," *The New York Times Magazine*, November 11, 2014.

11. Malcolm X, as told to Alex Haley, *The Autobiography of Malcolm X* (New York: Ballantine Books, 1965), 14. Page numbers correspond to the 2015 Ballantine Books Mass Market Edition.

12. Malcolm X, *The Autobiography*, 38.

13. Malcolm X, *The Autobiography*, 162–65.

14. Malcolm X, *The Autobiography*, 224.

15. Malcolm X, *The Autobiography*, 276.

16. Malcolm X, *The Autobiography*, 275.

17. Malcolm X, *The Autobiography*, 374.

18. George Wallace, Alabama gubernatorial inaugural address (Birmingham, Alabama), January 14, 1963, Alabama Department of Archives and History, http://digital.archives.alabama.gov/digital/collection/voices/id/2952.

19. John F. Kennedy, "Radio and Television Report to the American People on Civil Rights," June 11, 1963, Online by Gerhard Peters and John T. Woolley, The American Presidency Project, https://www.presidency.ucsb.edu/node/236675.

20. Malcolm X, *The Autobiography*, 369.

21. Lyndon B. Johnson, "Remarks at the University of Michigan," May 22, 1964, Online by Gerhard Peters and John T. Woolley, The American Presidency Project, https://www.presidency.ucsb.edu/node/239689.

22. Voting record on H.R. 7152, as provided by GovTrack, accessed August 31, 2020, https://www.govtrack.us/congress/votes/88-1964/s409, and https://www.govtrack.us/congress/votes/88-1964/h182.

23. Lyndon B. Johnson, "Special Message to the Congress: The American Promise," March 15, 1965, Online by Gerhard Peters and John T. Woolley, The American Presidency Project, https://www.presidency.ucsb.edu/node/242211.

24. Martin Luther King Jr., interview with Sander Vanocur of NBC News, May 8, 1967, accessed August 31, 2020, https://www.nbcnews.com/video/martin-luther-king-jr-speaks-with-nbc-news-11-months-before-assassination-1202163779741.

25. *Office of Management and Budget Historical Tables*, "Table 14.5: Total Government Expenditures by Major Category of Expenditure as Percentages of GDP: 1948–2019," Office of Management and Budget, https://www.whitehouse.gov/omb/historical-tables/.

26. *Office of Management and Budget Historical Tables*, "Table 1.2: Summary of Receipts, Outlays, and Surpluses or Deficits (-) as Percentages of GDP: 1930–2025," Office of Management and Budget.

27. Campbell Gibson and Kay Jung, *Historical Census Statistics on Population Totals by Race, 1790 to 1990, and by Hispanic Origin, 1970 to 1990, for the United States, Regions, Divisions, and States*, Working Paper No. 56, Population Division, US Census Bureau, (Washington, D.C.: 2002).

28. National Advisory Commission on Civil Disorders, *Report of the National Advisory Commission on Civil Disorders: Summary of Report* (Washington, D.C.: US Government Printing Office, 1968).

29. National Advisory Commission on Civil Disorders, *Summary of Report*.

30. Jeffrey Jones, "Americans Divided on Whether King's Dream Has Been Realized," *Gallup*, August 26, 2011, accessed August 31, 2020, https://news.gallup.com/poll/149201/americans-divided-whether-king-dream-realized.aspx.

Chapter 10: Drifting to Diversity

1. John F. Kennedy, *A Nation of immigrants* (New York: Harper & Row, 1964).
2. Kennedy, *A Nation of Immigrants*.
3. Lyndon B. Johnson, "Remarks at the Signing of the Immigration Bill, Liberty Island, New York," October 3, 1965, Online by Gerhard Peters and John T. Woolley, The American Presidency Project, https://www.presidency.ucsb.edu/node/241316.
4. Andrew Glass, "This Day in Politics: LBJ hails immigration reform, Oct. 3, 1965," *Politico*, October 3, 2018, accessed August 31, 2020, https://www.politico.com/story/2018/10/03/this-day-in-politics-october-3-854145.
5. Glass, "LBJ hails immigration reform."
6. Calculated from the 1970 Census as provided by IPUMS NHGIS.
7. Robert Pear, "President Signs Landmark Bill on Immigration," *New York Times*, November 7, 1986.
8. Pew Research Center estimates 10.5 million unauthorized immigrants lived in the United States as of 2017: Jeffrey S. Passel and D'Vera Cohn, "Mexicans decline to less than half the U.S. unauthorized immigrant population for the first time," Pew Research Center, June 12, 2019, accessed August 31, 2020, https://www.pewresearch.org/fact-tank/2019/06/12/us-unauthorized-immigrant-population-2017/.
9. The 55% in the footnote was calculated by aggregating annual data provided by the Department of Homeland Security. Citation for one example year, being 2017: *2017 Yearbook of Immigration Statistics*, "Table 11: Persons Obtaining Lawful Permanent Resident Status by Broad Class of Admission and Region and Country of Last Residence," Office of Immigration Statistics (Washington, D.C.: Government Printing Office, 2019).
10. *2017 Yearbook of Immigration Statistics*, "Table 2: Persons Obtaining Lawful Permanent Resident Status by Region and Selected Country of Last Residence: Fiscal Years 1820 to 2017," Office of Immigration Statistics (Washington, D.C.: Government Printing Office, 2019).
11. Department of Homeland Security, *Yearbook of Immigration Statistics*, aggregation of data across multiple years.
12. Department of Homeland Security, *2017 Yearbook of Immigration Statistics*.
13. 1970 data source: 1970 Census, US Census Bureau. 2019 data source: "QuickFacts," US Census Bureau, accessed August 31, 2020, https://www.census.gov/quickfacts.

Chapter 11: Coming Together

1. Lacking wealth data for 1970, I used 1963 data as a proxy. To determine 98% of wealth was held by White people, I applied 1960 Census population figures to 1963 average wealth by race. The latter was provided by: "Nine Charts about Wealth Inequality in America," Urban Institute, last updated October 5, 2017, https://apps.urban.org/features/wealth-inequality-charts/.

2. US Library of Congress, Congressional Research Service, *Federal Spending on Benefits and Services for People with Low Income: FY2008-2018 Update*, by Karen Lynch, Gene Falk, Jessica Tollestrup, Conor Boyle, and Patrick Landers, R46214 (2020), 4.

3. *Office of Management and Budget Historical Tables*, "Table 14.5—Total Government Expenditures by Major Category of Expenditure as Percentages of GDP: 1948–2019," Office of Management and Budget.

4. More precise estimates are 43% White, 42% Black, 8% Hispanic, 5% Asian, and 2% Other. Provided by: "QuickFacts," US Census Bureau, accessed August 31, 2020, https://www.census.gov/quickfacts.

5. Calculated from: *Vital Statistics on Congress*, The Brookings Institution.

6. *Historical Income Tables*, "Table F-5. Race and Hispanic Origin of Householder—Families by Median and Mean Income," US Census Bureau.

7. *Data Finder*, "Table 4: Life expectancy at birth," National Center for Health Statistics.

8. "How Groups Voted in 2008," Roper Center, accessed August 31, 2020, https://ropercenter.cornell.edu/how-groups-voted-2008.

Chapter 12: Staying Apart

1. Calculated from: *Vital Statistics on Congress*, The Brookings Institution.

2. Minority % in Congress calculated from: *Vital Statistics on Congress*, The Brookings Institution. Minority % of the population, years 2010 and prior, calculated from: Decennial US censuses, US Census Bureau. Minority % of the population for 2020 reflects an estimate as of July 1, 2019, provided by: "QuickFacts," US Census Bureau, accessed August 31, 2020, https://www.census.gov/quickfacts.

3. *Understanding Fair Housing*, US Commission on Civil Rights, (Washington D.C.: US Government Printing Office, 1973).

4. Map data reflects the 1970 Census and the 2017 American Community Survey (used as a proxy for 2020) provided by IPUMS NHGIS. Shapefiles to create the map were also provided by IPUMS NHGIS.

5. Data points for all years are shown in constant 2018 dollars, as provided by: *Historical Income Tables*, "Table F-5. Race and Hispanic Origin of Householder—Families by Median and Mean Income," US Census Bureau.

6. "Nine Charts about Wealth Inequality in America," Urban Institute.

7. Data for years 1970–2010 came from US censuses provided by IPUMS NHGIS. Data for year 2020 came from: "Quarterly Residential Vacancies and Homeownership, Second Quarter 2020," Social, Economic, & Housing Statistics Division of the US Census Bureau, release number CB20-107, July 28, 2020.

8. *Digest of Education Statistics, 2018*, "Table 226.10 – Number, percentage distribution, and SAT mean scores of high school seniors taking the SAT, by sex, race/ethnicity, first language learned, and highest level of parental education: 2017 and 2018," National Center for Education Statistics, https://nces.ed.gov/programs/digest/2018menu_tables.asp.

9. *CPS Historical Time Series Tables*, "Table A-2," US Census Bureau.

10. *Historical Poverty Tables: People and Families–1959 to 2018*, "Table 2. Poverty Status of People by Family Relationship, Race, and Hispanic Origin," US Census Bureau, https://www.census.gov/data/tables/time-series/demo/income-poverty/historical-poverty-people.html.

11. Richard Nixon, "War on Drugs Speech," June 17, 1971, https://www.nixonfoundation.org/2016/06/26404/.

12. Ronald and Nancy Reagan, "Address to the Nation on the Campaign Against Drug Abuse," September 14, 1986, Online by Gerhard Peters and John T. Woolley, The American Presidency Project, https://www.presidency.ucsb.edu/node/254374.

13. Ronald Reagan, "Remarks on Signing the Anti-Drug Abuse Act of 1986," October 27, 1986, Online by Gerhard Peters and John T. Woolley, The American Presidency Project, https://www.presidency.ucsb.edu/node/254289.

14. People of Hispanic ethnicity are excluded from the White, Black, and Asian datapoints. Data source: WONDER Online Database, Centers for Disease Control and Prevention (CDC), http://wonder.cdc.gov.

15. People of Hispanic ethnicity are excluded from the White and Black bars. Data for the Asian bar was not available. Data for the graph was calculated from Tables 5, 14, and 16 of the following report: Ann E. Carson, "Prisoners in 2018," US Department of Justice, Bureau of Justice Statistics, April 2020, NCJ 253516, https://www.bjs.gov/content/pub/pdf/p18.pdf.

16. Barack Obama, "Address at the National Constitution Center in Philadelphia: 'A More Perfect Union,'" March 18, 2008, Online by Gerhard Peters and John T. Woolley, The American Presidency Project, https://www.presidency.ucsb.edu/node/277610.

17. Barack Obama, "A More Perfect Union."

Appendix: Defining Race

1. Office of Management and Budget, "Revisions to the Standards for the Classification of Federal Data on Race and Ethnicity," *Federal Register* 62, no. 210 (October 30, 1997): 5872–90, https://www.govinfo.gov/content/pkg/FR-1997-10-30/pdf/97-28653.pdf.

2. "Index of Questions," US Census Bureau, https://www.census.gov/history/www/through_the_decades/index_of_questions/.

3. *Ninth Census of the United States, Instructions to Assistant Marshalls*, Census Office, Department of the Interior, (Washington: Government Printing Office, 1870), 10–11.

4. *Eleventh Census of the United States, Instructions to Assistant Marshalls*, Census Office, Department of the Interior, (Washington: Government Printing Office, 1890), 23.

5. "Index of Questions," US Census Bureau.